The
Antichrist and
the Mark of
the Beast

Larry W. Wilson

Copyright © 2021

Wake Up America Seminars, Inc.
P.O. Box 273, Bellbrook, Ohio 45305
(800) 475-0876

ISBN 978-0-9848102-0-8

First edition, April 2021

All rights reserved.

On occasion, italics and brackets in Scripture quotations have been added to enhance understanding. They are not intended to change the meaning of the texts, only to clarify. We encourage you to consider them and hope they will provide you with deeper insight as you study God's Word.

The Antichrist and The Mark of the Beast

Who is the Antichrist?

For more than 500 years, people have speculated and prognosticated over the identity of the Antichrist. Since medieval times, Protestants have claimed it was a particular pope or the Office of the Pope. Others have said he will be a European-born man who gains control over the United Nations. Some believe it is the president of the United States. Previously, others thought he was Mikhail Gorbachev, Adolph Hitler, Napoleon Bonaparte, or Nero. There has been endless confusion on the identity of the Antichrist because it was not time for the truth to be known—until now.

God has a consistent mechanism that terminates prophetic speculation. When the time arrives for Bible prophecy to be fulfilled, those seeking truth discover the intended meaning of His Word! "Progressive revelation" makes this possible and the result becomes "present truth." Present truth is like a seed that lies dormant beneath the surface and when the time is right, it springs up! Paul's ministry was based on "progressive revelation" which produced "present truth." Consider his words: **"The message I proclaim about Jesus Christ, [is] in keeping with the revelation of the mystery *hidden for long ages past, but now revealed and made known* through the prophetic writings by the command of the eternal God."**[1]

We also find "progressive revelation" in the book of Daniel. God sealed the book of Daniel until the time of the end.[2] Now that the four rules governing prophetic interpretation have been discovered, *present truth* has appeared! God has provided this present truth about the identity of the Antichrist to the final generation so those who have ears to hear can be prepared.

---

1   Romans 16:25-26, insertion and italics mine
2   Daniel 12:4, 9

The Bible teaches the coming Antichrist will be a fallen angel. He is the devil—also called Satan. He was the first to become anti-Christ and he will be the last angel burning in hell. To date, Joseph Stalin is credited with killing over 6 million people during his regime; and Mao Zedong is said to have killed around 42 million Chinese during his reign. Compared to those two, Adolf Hitler was an amateur. However, when the Antichrist appears, he will be the worst nightmare the world has ever experienced. He will kill more people than all the other tyrants in history!

People will see the devil and his demons because at God's appointed time, He will give them physical bodies! Masquerading as the glorious almighty God, the devil will deceive billions of people with miracles, signs, and wonders. He will call fire down from heaven at will to confirm his lies and empty promises.

After the Antichrist does a five-month charade of traveling the world, healing the sick, feeding the hungry, and performing miracles and amazing wonders, he will gain enough believers to turn the world upside down. At a precise point in time (hour, day, month, and year), Jesus will allow the devil to impose demonic authority over the entire world. The Antichrist will abolish all governments and religions to set up a new global government and worldwide religion. Circumstances will be dire: Obey and live or disobey and die.

The Antichrist will promise a thousand years of peace and prosperity, but his kingdom instead will be endless exhaustion, sorrow, and suffering. He will put to death anyone who refuses to obey his cruel orders if captured. The Bible says the Antichrist will kill *one-third* of mankind![1] The Antichrist will have no regard for man's laws. Even worse, mankind cannot contain, stop, or kill him.

The following sentence may not seem important, but think about this: *God took the form of "a man" to save the world; God will permit the devil to take the form of "a man" to destroy it.*

---

1   Revelation 9:15

Why God Permits the Antichrist to Appear

The Bible declares that God is love and changeless. This changeless God of love destroyed all but eight people with a flood in Noah's day. How do we reconcile His actions with His character? The Bible answers: **"The Lord saw how great the wickedness of the human race had become on the earth, and that every inclination of the thoughts of the human heart was only evil all the time. The Lord regretted that he had made human beings on the earth, and his heart was deeply troubled. So the Lord said, 'I will wipe from the face of the earth the human race I have created – and with them the animals, the birds and the creatures that move along the ground – for I regret that I have made them.' But Noah found favor in the eyes of the Lord."**[1]

About five hundred years after Noah's flood, the Bible indicates that God destroyed Sodom and Gomorrah for the same reason He destroyed the world in Noah's day: **"Now the people of Sodom were wicked and were sinning greatly against the Lord."**[2] Jumping forward to the end of the age, a changeless God of love will destroy wicked people at the end of the one thousand years. In fact, the Bible says, **"In number they** [the wicked] **are like the sand on the seashore."**[3]

Contrary to what scoffers say, God is not a tyrant; He is not arbitrary or cruel. God loves people more deeply than we can love anyone, even our own children. Although many people do not understand God's reasons, He sent His Son to the cross to redeem repentant sinners! Scoffers do not understand what a changeless God of love has to deal with. The sinful nature of man is a pattern all societies follow.

God loves oncoming generations just as much as He loves the present one. When a generation or group of people becomes decadent, defiant, violent, and sexually immoral, God knows the

1   Genesis 6:5-8
2   Genesis 13:13
3   Revelation 20:8, insertion mine

following generation will be worse because the curse of sin does this to humanity. To end the downward spiral that wickedness produces, God ends decadent behavior with destruction. It may come through water as in Noah's day, or fire as with Sodom and Gomorrah; it may come through God's four judgments of sword, famine, plague, and wild beasts;[1] or it may come through a person whom God empowers as a destroyer.

God used Jonah to warn of coming destruction. **"Go to the great city of Nineveh and preach against it, because its wickedness has come up before me"[2] "Now Nineveh was a very large city; it took three days to go through it. Jonah began by going a day's journey into the city, proclaiming, 'Forty more days and Nineveh will be overthrown.'"[3]** Even though that generation repented, subsequent generations returned to their wicked ways.[4]

God responded by sending King Nebuchadnezzar to destroy that huge city. God also used King Nebuchadnezzar to destroy Jerusalem and His own people! The Lord even calls the pagan king *my servant*: **"'I will summon all the peoples of the north and *my servant* Nebuchadnezzar king of Babylon,' declares the Lord, 'and I will bring them against this land [Judea] and its inhabitants and against all the surrounding nations. I will completely destroy them and make them an object of horror and scorn, and an everlasting ruin.'"[5]** In the same manner, God later raised King Cyrus and King Darius to destroy Babylon.[6] Later still, God raised up Alexander the Great to destroy the Persian Empire.[7]

There are several Bible examples in which God empowered a person as His destroyer. A changeless God of love hates to do this, but He loves oncoming generations as much as the present generation. When a group of people reach a point in decadence and

1   Ezekiel 14:21
2   Jonah 1:2
3   Jonah 3:3-4
4   Nahum 1:14
5   Jeremiah 25:9; see also Leviticus 26:27-35, insertion and italics mine
6   Jeremiah 25:12; Isaiah 45:1
7   Daniel 8:20-21

defiance and when God's extended mercy has no redeeming effect, He can only send destruction. This will be the situation when the Antichrist appears. God's continued mercy is pointless, so He will release the devil and his demons from the Abyss (the spirit realm). God's primary purpose for releasing a worldwide destroyer will be the destruction of everything that mankind has created: **"They** [the demons] **had *as king over them the angel of the Abyss*, whose name in Hebrew is Abaddon and in Greek is Apollyon (that is,** [for Jew and Gentile alike, his name means] **Destroyer)."**[1]

A Fallen Angel Will Appear as a Man!

It may seem strange that the devil is the Antichrist and will physically appear in the form of *a man* during the Great Tribulation. If the Bible did not teach this, I would not believe it; but Isaiah declares the devil's origin, deeds, and fate. Isaiah speaks as though he is observing the devil at the end of the age when the devil is destroyed. This perspective is important because at that time, and only at that time, will everyone actually see the devil. The only generation that sees the devil and his demons in physical form is the final generation.

Isaiah begins: **"How you have fallen from heaven, morning star, son of the dawn! You have been cast down to the earth, you who once laid low the nations!**[2] Isaiah is struck by the heighth and depth of the devil's experience. The devil lived in heaven before he was cast out. He is called **"son of the dawn"** because he was the first created being. He is called **"morning star"** because he was the brightest and most gifted angel. Isaiah continues: **"you who once laid low the nations."** This language indicates this fallen angel destroyed the nations of the world. Daniel adds, **"He will cause astounding devastation and will succeed in whatever he does."**[3]

---

1   Revelation 9:11, insertions and italics mine
2   Isaiah 14:12
3   Daniel 8:24

This is not surprising, for John wrote in Revelation 9:11, his name means destroyer. God reveals the devil's thoughts and motives through Isaiah: **"You said in your heart, 'I will ascend to the heavens; I will raise my throne above the stars of God; I will sit enthroned on the mount of assembly, on the utmost heights of Mount Zaphon.** [This mountain is also known as Jebel Aqra and has long been regarded as sacred. It is located on the border with Turkey and Syria and has an elevation of 5,633 feet. In ancient times, the Canaanites believed the "storm god" lived at the top of this mountain from where destruction originated.] **I will ascend above the tops of the clouds; I will make myself like the Most High.'"**[1] More than anything, the devil wants the rights and prerogatives that belong only to God almighty.

Isaiah explains his fate: **"But you** [son of the dawn, who aspired to raise your throne above the stars of God and make yourself like the Most High] **are brought down to the realm of the dead, to the depths of the pit.** [In other words, this mighty and gifted angel can sink no lower physically or in esteem. He is thrown into the pit (a mass grave) with the rest of God's enemies.] **Those who see you stare at you, they ponder your fate: 'Is this *the man* who shook the earth and made kingdoms tremble, *the man* who made the world a wilderness, who overthrew its cities and would not let his captives go home?' "**[2]

These sentences bring several facts together. First, Isaiah describes an angel who was the first to be created, whose gifts and abilities made him the brightest star, and who once lived in heaven. This angel shook the earth, made kingdoms tremble, overthrew cities, and made it a wilderness. Although a supernatural being, he is mortal and he is **"brought down to the realm of the dead."** At the end of the age, when everyone can stare at him, they ask twice, **"Is this *the man*?"** because the devil will be in the form of a man! The phrase, he **"would not let his captives go home"** means that during his reign of terror, he will not release anyone from the prison he creates.

---

1   Isaiah 14:13-14, insertion mine
2   Isaiah 14:15-17, insertions and italics mine

When God permits the devil and his demons to appear, their mission will be death and destruction. The Bible gives us advance notice: They plan to kill the saints, torture their captives, and destroy the world.

If there is any doubt remaining about the identity of the Antichrist, Ezekiel should put it to rest. To begin, notice that Ezekiel's comments are directed toward the *authentic ruler* of the wicked city of Tyre. When God gave this prophecy, the visible ruler of Tyre was merely the devil's hand puppet. The Lord saw the devil's success in leading this great city into wickedness. Therefore the Lord directed His comments to the *authentic ruler* of Tyre (the devil).

"Son of man, say to the [authentic] ruler of Tyre, 'This is what the Sovereign Lord says: "In the pride of your heart you say, 'I am a god; I sit on the throne of a god in the heart of the seas.' [A phrase meaning, "adored in the hearts of the people."] **But you are a mere mortal and not a god, though you think you are as wise as a god." ' "**[1]

The Lord reminded the devil that he is not a god; he is a mere mortal. The devil cannot keep himself alive. Only deities have the power to live endlessly and to give life. The Lord condemned the devil's arrogance saying, **"You think you are as wise as a god."** If the devil were as wise as he thinks, he would not have chosen the course of hatred and rebellion, because his destruction is certain and inescapable.

"You were anointed as a guardian cherub, for so I ordained you. You were on the holy mount of God; you walked among the fiery stones. You were blameless in your ways from the day you were created till wickedness was found in you."[2] The Lord reminded the devil that he was created blameless, but over time chose to become evil. He deliberately and defiantly made decisions that resulted in his eviction from heaven. Even though all beings start off blameless, we

1   Ezekiel 28:2, insertions mine
2   Ezekiel 28:14-15

are accountable to God for our choices and conduct! Our response to the Holy Spirit determines our eternal destiny.

"Through your widespread trade you were filled with violence, and you sinned. So I drove you in disgrace from the mount of God, and I expelled you, guardian cherub, from among the fiery stones."[1] The devil and his angels were humiliated when God expelled them from heaven. Even though the devil was a guardian cherub (the highest position in heaven that a created being could have), his position meant nothing when wickedness overcame him.

"Your heart became proud on account of your beauty, and you corrupted your wisdom because of your splendor. So I threw you to the earth; I made a spectacle of you before kings. By your many sins and dishonest trade you have desecrated your sanctuaries."[2] The devil was the first angel created; he was also the most gifted. His beauty, talents, and position were above the rest. Jesus confronted the devil with his disaffection and rebellion many times before he was cast out of heaven. This is why the devil hates Christ with a passion. The devil was the first to become anti-Christ and his hatred has been all-consuming for 6,000 years. He is condemned because he has used his great powers and evil influence to contaminate and attempt to ruin both heaven and Earth (his sanctuaries – his dwelling places).

"So I made a fire come out from you, and it consumed you, and I reduced you to ashes on the ground in the sight of all who were watching. All the nations who knew you are appalled at you; you have come to a horrible end and will be no more."[3]

God has specific punishment for Lucifer at the end of the 1,000 years. He will be burned with fire expanding and engulfing from within. He will suffer according to the amount of suffering he has caused. His end will be horrible and after justice has been served, the devil will be no more. **" 'Surely the day is coming; it will burn like**

1   Ezekiel 28:16
2   Ezekiel 28:17-18
3   Ezekiel 28:18-19

a furnace. **All the arrogant and every evildoer will be stubble, and the day that is coming will set them on fire,' says the Lord Almighty. 'Not a root or a branch will be left to them.' "**[1]

Through the ages, God used the desires of kings to accomplish His purposes. For example, King Nebuchadnezzar wanted to destroy the governments of Nineveh, Tyre, and Jerusalem so that his authority would be absolute. Cyrus and Darius destroyed the government of Babylon so their authority would be absolute. God will release the devil and his demons from the Abyss allowing Satan to do what he has wanted to do for 6,000 years. Satan wants to rule the world, so he and his demons will abolish the governments of the world, kill the saints, and torture the captives. Jesus, who is now holding the devil back, will release a worldwide destroyer when the appointed time arrives. **"And now you know what is holding him back, so that he may be revealed at the proper time."**[2]

When Will the Antichrist Appear?

Before the Antichrist appears, a great enlightenment will occur around the world. During the Great Tribulation, God will send four testing messages throughout the earth. He will pour the Holy Spirit out on all people[3] and speak through His servants, the 144,000. Each nation, kindred, tongue, and people will hear these four messages. The messages will weigh heavily on each heart as the Holy Spirit makes them pivotal. I use the word "pivotal" to indicate everyone will either turn to God in genuine repentance and submission *or* turn against Him. These four messages will tear families, cities, and nations apart. Jesus said, **"And everyone who has left houses or brothers or sisters or father or mother or wife or children or fields for my sake will receive a hundred times as much and will inherit eternal life."**[4] Understanding this coming truth is important because God will use it to separate the "sheep" from the "goats." Those who love God and His truth will suffer persecution. Those

1   Malachi 4:1
2   2 Thessalonians 2:6
3   Joel 2:28-30
4   Matthew 19:29

who refuse to obey the four messages will become furious with the 144,000 and individuals who align with them because people who disobey will be filled with defiance and rebellion.

Paul indicates the rebellion will occur before a diabolical *man* appears: **"Don't let anyone deceive you in any way, for that day** [the Second Coming] **will not come** [a] *until the rebellion occurs* **and** [b] *the man of lawlessness is revealed*, **the man doomed to destruction. He will oppose and will exalt himself over everything that is called God or is worshiped, so that he sets himself up in God's temple, proclaiming himself to be God."**[1]

Consider the five specifications Paul gives in these two verses. First, the title for this man is paramount. He will be a lawless *man*. He will not respect the laws of man. He will do as he pleases because he knows no one is powerful enough to stop him. Second, he will seem to be indestructible, but he will be destroyed after he has served his purpose. Daniel adds to this: **"He will become very strong, but not by his own power. He will cause astounding devastation and will succeed in whatever he does. He will destroy those who are mighty, the holy people** [the 144,000]. **He will cause deceit to prosper, and he will consider himself superior. When they feel secure, he will destroy many and take his stand against the Prince of princes** [Jesus]. **Yet he will be destroyed,** *but not by human power.***"**[2]

Third, Paul says the man of lawlessness will **"oppose and exalt himself over everything that is called God or is worshiped."** The man of lawlessness will *oppose* the religions of the world such as Catholicism, Islam, Hinduism, Protestantism, and Judaism. He will oppose them because he will set up his own religion. He will also abolish the governments of the world because his laws and powers are above the laws and powers of mankind. Fourth, he will set himself up in God's temple demanding worship that belongs to God. Last, he will proclaim himself to be God. This final specification

1   2 Thessalonians 2:3-4, insertions and italics mine
2   Daniel 8:24-25, insertions and italics mine

explains the previous specifications. The man of lawlessness will masquerade as almighty God. He will have powers and abilities that human beings do not possess!

Paul continues: **"The coming of the lawless one will be** [brilliant and glorious, like the Second Coming, but it will be a great deception, this is] **in accordance with how Satan works. He will use all sorts of displays of power through signs and wonders that serve the lie** [that he is God]**, and** [he will use] **all the ways that wickedness deceives those who are perishing. They perish because they** [heard the four messages delivered by the 144,000, but] **refused to love the truth and so be saved. For this reason God sends them a powerful delusion** [the delusion is the man of lawlessness who masquerades as almighty God] **so that they will believe the lie and so that all will be condemned who have not believed the truth but have delighted in wickedness."**[1]

The Antichrist Appears at the Fifth Trumpet

The prophet John saw seven angels standing before God and seven trumpets were given to them.[2] John says when the fifth angel sounds his trumpet, the Antichrist will appear![3] Although the Bible tells us the Antichrist will appear at the fifth trumpet, the knowledge is not helpful if we have no idea when the fifth trumpet will occur. God has a reason for obscuring when the Antichrist will appear because He wants to surprise people who rejected the testimony of the 144,000. In fact, He wants the appearing of the Antichrist to be a powerful delusion.

It may seem inconsistent that a God of love would send a powerful delusion so wicked people will believe a lie; but once you understand the circumstances, it makes sense! Consider this Bible example: If God had wanted to save the world in Noah's day, He could have left the door of the ark open for a few hours *after* it began to rain. As it was, the door closed *before* the rain began because God had

---

1   2 Thessalonians 2:9-12, insertions mine
2   Revelation 8:2
3   Revelation 9:1-11

warned the people through His servant Noah for 120 years. Salvation always requires faith in God and a love for His truth!

Consider the world in Noah's day from God's point of view: **"The Lord saw how great the wickedness of the human race had become on the earth, and that every inclination of the thoughts of the human heart was only evil all the time. The Lord regretted that he had made human beings on the earth, and his heart was deeply troubled."**[1] God is responsible for the presence of human beings on Earth. He created us in His image and He sustains life. We cannot keep ourselves alive. He loves us and has given us free will with the power of choice. He has given us righteous laws and high standards by which to live so purpose and happiness fill our lives. When human beings become evil and violent, willfully and knowingly rejecting the clearest evidence of God's will, His only solution is to destroy them. This principle explains the flood and why God will permit the Antichrist to ruin cities, make the world a wilderness, and kill one third of mankind before the Second Coming!

During the Great Tribulation, God will reveal His will to everyone through His servants, the 144,000. Most people will not submit to God's requirements but will rebel (the great rebellion). After a period of grace, when God determines extended mercy has no redeeming effect, He will release the Antichrist. God knows that by releasing the Antichrist, a few wicked people will come to repentance and be saved after seeing evil incarnate. Current illustrations of man's inhumanity to man is nothing compared with the cruel and revolting ways of the devil and his demons.

Loving truth is extremely important to God, but it does not normally appeal to our sinful nature. The Holy Spirit creates a love for truth within us when we are born again. A humble spirit, a teachable attitude, and an honest heart are prerequisites for finding truth. God chose Noah to warn the world of a coming flood. 2 Peter 2:5 says that Noah was a preacher of righteousness. Genesis 6:3 says the Lord told Noah He was only going to tolerate humankind's

1   Genesis 6:5-6

wickedness for 120 more years. I believe Noah told the world *when* the flood was coming because he knew the year. However, people treated his message with contempt and went about their activities. Jesus predicted a parallel: **"For in the days before the flood, people were eating and drinking, marrying and giving in marriage, up to the day Noah entered the ark; and they knew nothing about what would happen until the flood came and took them all away. That is how it will be at the coming of the Son of Man."**[1]

Unseen Angels Are Everywhere

We may not be aware of their presence, but angels from heaven and the Abyss surround us. We do not see them because God keeps them out of sight.[2] Most Christians do not anticipate seeing the devil in the form of a glorious man, but 'supernatural' will become the norm when God allows the Antichrist to appear. Many biblical accounts about angelic appearances illustrate this point:

    • Hagar, the mother of Ishmael, saw an angel.[3]

1.   Abraham saw three angels in the form of three men.[4]
2.   Jacob saw an angel in the form of a man.[5]
3.   Moses saw an angel.[6]
4.   Balaam and Balaam's donkey saw an angel.[7]
5.   Gideon saw an angel.[8]
6.   Elijah saw an angel.[9]
7.   Araunah, his four sons, and King David saw an angel.[10]
8.   Daniel saw an angel.[11]
9.   Zechariah, a priest, saw an angel.[12]

---

1   Matthew 24:38-39
2   Hebrews 1:14; 1 Peter 5:8
3   Genesis 16
4   Genesis 18
5   Genesis 32
6   Exodus 3
7   Numbers 22
8   Judges 6
9   2 Kings 1
10   1 Chronicles 21
11   Daniel 9
12   Luke 1

10.   Peter saw an angel.[1]
11.   John saw an angel.[2]
12.   The whole camp of Israel saw and heard an angel![3]

The Angel King from the Abyss Appears!

When the fifth trumpet sounds, the whole world will see the angel king from the Abyss.* He is the Antichrist who will claim to be God, and he will turn the world upside down. He will oppose and abolish the religions and governments of the world. He will destroy cities and make the world a wilderness. The book of Revelation describes the devil as the beast from the Abyss![4]

* **Note:** God used "the Abyss" (bottomless pit, KJV) to describe the spirit realm. The ancients thought Earth was a flat plate. If a person dug a water well too deep, he would create a bottomless pit and fall into the Abyss. The ancients believed that demons lived beneath the earth and volcanos were chimneys proving that a perpetual fire burned under the earth. God used these images when He gave the Patmos vision to John and the language works perfectly well once you understand these ancient ideas.

Consider the angel's testimony to John: "[John,] **The beast, which you saw** [earlier in Chapter 12], [when Satan was represented as a great red dragon, at war with Michael in heaven. The beast was thrown out of heaven and cast into the earth. It] **once was** [visible] **now is not** [visible, because it was cast into the Abyss–the spirit realm], **and yet** [it, the great red dragon] **will come up out of the Abyss and go to its destruction.** [However, before the beast is destroyed,] **The inhabitants of the earth whose names have not been written in the book of life from the creation of the world** [that is, wicked people] **will be astonished** [surprised, overwhelmed] **when they** [actually] **see the beast** [because it will be the great red dragon in the form of a glorious man. The wicked will be caught

---

1   Acts 12
2   Revelation 19
3   Judges 2
4   Revelation 17:8

off guard], **because it** [the beast] **once was** [visible], **now is not** [visible], **and yet will come** [out of the Abyss – the spirit realm and be plainly visible!].**"**[1]

The wicked will be astonished when they literally see the man of lawlessness. His incredible glory and endless miracles, signs, and wonders will convince the wicked that God lives among men. Paul warned, **"The coming of the lawless one will be in accordance with how Satan works. He will use all sorts of displays of power through signs and wonders that serve the lie** [that he is God]**, and** [he will use] **all the ways that wickedness deceives those who are perishing. They perish because *they refused to love the truth* and so be saved. *For this reason God sends them a powerful delusion so that they will believe the lie* and so that all will be condemned who have not believed the truth but have delighted in wickedness."**[2]

Very few anticipate seeing a demon from the Abyss even though we just reviewed the texts where individuals actually saw angels. For centuries, people have argued over the identity of the Antichrist, never entertaining the idea he could, or would, be a superior being to a human. When God wants people to see, He opens their eyes; and when the time is right, the whole world will see the angel of the Abyss![3] Ages ago, God set the date when the Antichrist is to appear.

Satan Sets Himself Up in God's Temple

Paul says the man of lawlessness will set himself up in God's temple. Many people interpret these words to mean the temple in Jerusalem will be rebuilt. Paul's words do not support this anticipation. God sealed Temple Mount in the seventh century by giving it to the Muslims.

Paul speaks about a situation much larger and more important than Temple Mount. Isaiah, David, John, and Paul understood that God's throne is *within* His temple.[4] This arrangement produces a perfect church/state (theocracy) where God is both King of kings and Lord

---

1 Revelation 17:8, insertions mine
2 2 Thessalonians 2:9-12, insertions and italics mine
3 Revelation 9:11
4 Isaiah 6:1, Psalm 11:4-5 and Revelation 7:15

of lords. He rules as king from His throne and is worshiped as God in His temple. His authority and truth go out from His throne which is in His temple.

Paul predicts the man of lawlessness will set up a throne and rule over Earth as its king demanding worship that belongs to God. The result will be a counterfeit theocracy. Because the devil will be *opposed* to all that is worshiped or called God, he will have zero interest in Jerusalem or Israel. He will also have zero interest in Mecca, Vatican City, or Washington, D.C. The Antichrist and his demons will be traveling constantly. The Bible teaches the throne and temple of the Father is not located at a fixed address.[1] In like manner, the throne and temple of the Antichrist will be wherever he is. The devil and his demons will appear anywhere at any time because of their supernatural power.[2]

God Has Set the Exact Time

Consider the timing of the sixth trumpet: **"The sixth angel sounded his trumpet, and I heard a voice . . . It said . . . 'Release the four angels who are bound at the great river Euphrates.' And the four angels who had been kept ready for this very hour and day and month and year were released to kill a third of mankind."**[3] Because God has set the date for the sixth trumpet by His sovereign authority,[4] it is reasonable to conclude God has also set the date for the fifth trumpet because the fifth trumpet lasts for five months before the sixth trumpet.[5] Of course, God has set the dates for all the events that will occur during Earth's final days.

God has yet to reveal the hour, day, month, and year when the Antichrist will appear, but I believe the 144,000 will announce his appearance so the saints will be prepared. Even though the Bible does not give the specific date, we can narrow down the time.

---

1   Ezekiel 1; Revelation 21:22
2   Ephesians 2:2; Revelation 9:3
3   Revelation 9:13-15
4   Acts 1:7
5   Revelation 9:10

Contemplate these four points:

1. God has set the dates for the fifth and sixth trumpet.

2. The fifth trumpet occurs after the fourth trumpet.

3. Paul says the wicked refused to love the truth. This indicates the whole world had an opportunity to hear the truth. Given the global destruction caused by the first four trumpets, it will take time for the 144,000 to present God's truth to survivors on Earth.

4. A worldwide rebellion must occur before the Antichrist appears. Daniel says, **"When rebels have become completely wicked, a fierce-looking king, a master of intrigue, will arise."**[1]

God's Ways

One day, **"The disciples came to him [Jesus] and asked, 'Why do you speak to the people in parables?' He replied, 'Because the knowledge of the secrets of the kingdom of heaven has been given to you, but not to them.'"**[2] Jesus hid the secrets of the kingdom of heaven for two reasons. First, if Jesus spoke clearly about the requirements for the kingdom, the truth would have made the Jews furious and they would have tried to kill Him prematurely. In fact, this almost happened![3] Jesus summarized the importance of being discreet with truth saying, **"Do not give dogs what is sacred; do not throw your pearls to pigs. If you do, they may trample them under their feet, and turn and tear you to pieces."**[4] More importantly, the Father reveals truth to those who hunger and thirst for righteousness. Jesus said, **"Blessed are those who hunger and thirst for righteousness, for they will be filled."**[5]

The Father seeks a certain type of person for the kingdom of heaven Jesus said, **"Blessed are the meek, for they will inherit the earth."**[6]

---

1   Daniel 8:23
2   Matthew 13:10-11, insertion mine
3   Luke 4:29
4   Matthew 7:6
5   Matthew 5:6
6   Matthew 5:5

Blessed are the pure in heart, for they will see God."[1] "True worshipers will worship the Father in the *Spirit and in truth*, for they are the kind of worshipers the Father seeks. God is [humble in] spirit, and his worshipers must worship in the [same humble] Spirit and in truth."[2] The Father requires a particular kind of people in the kingdom of heaven. The Antichrist's miracles, signs, and wonders will not deceive them. Jesus said, "A wicked and adulterous generation asks for a sign!"[3] Jesus said this because a miracle is a show of power, but a show of power does not change the heart! King Pharaoh saw ten miracles that did not change his heart. The Pharisees saw Jesus perform many miracles that did not change their hearts. The Antichrist knows this very well since he used this principle when he ruled over Pharaoh and the Pharisees. Therefore, the devil will provide many signs and wonders to satisfy people controlled by their sinful nature. Satan will deceive and sooth the conscience of billions of people, convincing them the 144,000 are demon possessed! Jesus warned, "For false messiahs and false prophets will appear and perform great signs and wonders to deceive, if possible, even the elect [those who know better]."[4] When right becomes wrong and wrong becomes right, the ultimate deception has occurred.

God's ways can seem strange at first, but when viewed in reverse, they always make sense. God arranged circumstances in Noah's day so that salvation from the flood was a test of faith. God sent a messenger with a *timely* announcement and He tested the inhabitants of Earth to see who would love truth. Even the miracle of seeing wild animals calmly file into the ark, two-by-two (unclean animals), and in groups of seven (clean animals), did not convince the people! All but eight people drowned. Even the men who helped build the boat, other than Noah's sons, failed the test of faith.

Now, I am speculating that men other than Noah's sons helped build this enormous ship. The Bible does not address this point, but it would

---

1   Matthew 5:8
2   John 4:23-24, insertions and italics mine
3   Matthew 12:39
4   Matthew 24:24, insertion mine

have taken many men to build this great ark. During construction, many men entered the ark to make the stalls and accommodations; however, entering the ark for wages and entering because of faith are very different motives. Unfortunately, the same thing is about to happen again. God will set up circumstances for a test of faith.[1] He will send 144,000 messengers throughout the world with timely declarations. The Bible predicts a huge number of people will forfeit salvation because they do not love truth.

The Great Tribulation Begins

I would like to present an idea that may be helpful in understanding when the Antichrist, the man of lawlessness, the beast from the Abyss, will appear. Given the nature of this idea, understand that a world of difference exists between time study and date setting. God has placed eighteen prophetic time periods in the books of Daniel and Revelation; correct alignment is essential to know God's plans. Aligning these prophetic time periods is time study. Date setting, on the other hand, is a fool's errand.

I believe the Great Tribulation will begin during the next worldwide war, World War III. After warring nations have killed millions of people in nuclear exchanges, Jesus will suddenly step into the war with firepower so great, it will arrest the attention survivors and cause the war to cease! When the whole world is praying for peace and safety, Jesus will send sudden destruction.[2] His display of divine power and His forthcoming judgments will result in the Great Tribulation.

The Bible teaches God's wrath will begin the Great Tribulation. Day One of the Great Tribulation will be marked by physical signs in the heavens and in the earth.[3] There will be enormous bolts of lightning from the sky to Earth and from horizon to horizon. There will be intimidating peals of thunder. There will be voices coming out of the earth. A global earthquake will tear apart power grids, runways,

1   Revelation 3:10
2   1 Thessalonians 5:3
3   Revelation 8:5

train tracks, and bridges. Everyone on Earth will tremble when a small sample of God's wrath is released on Day One.

Then, a meteoric firestorm will occur burning one third of the earth! Two civilization-threatening asteroid impacts will follow. The first asteroid will impact an ocean and the resulting tsunami will destroy thousands of coastal cities around the rim of the ocean. The second asteroid will impact a continent, shearing its geologic strata. Underground aquifers will be contaminated by sewage and buried waste. Poisoned water will be widely transported by underground rivers and millions of people will die from drinking the water, even though they live long distances from ground zero.

Later, the "Ring of Fire" around the Pacific Ocean will come to life and many volcanos will spew dust and soot into the atmosphere. The jet stream will transport this debris around the middle third of Earth and cause global darkness and famine. Subsequently, the devil's miracles will be so effective at the fifth trumpet when he heals the sick and feeds millions of starving people!

Revelation 6:7-8 says one fourth of Earth's population (~2 billion people) will die during the first four trumpets after the Lamb breaks the fourth seal. I understand these four judgments will occur over a period of about 65 days. To say that God's wrath will traumatize the world is a gross understatement. Religious and political leaders, and others who have no clue about the fulfillment of Revelation 8 will be extremely frightened and shocked with Jesus' display of sovereign power.

Fear of God will overwhelm billions of people. Religious people will say, "This is the wrath of almighty God" especially since the 144,000 declare the information from Revelation 8 which describes *the order of the four judgments* which have destroyed notably wicked places! When tribulation, fear, darkness, suffering, and sorrow fill each passing hour, a new reality occurs. These judgments will be off the scale in comparison to previous world wars; the amount of destruction and fear is mind-boggling. As misery within every nation increases, leaders will not escape the evidence: Almighty God is angry with the whole world.

God's wrath will come in two phases. The first phase contains mercy. Individuals can repent and be saved. The second phase has no mercy. The wicked will commit the unpardonable sin and receive the mark of the beast. For reasons beyond the scope of this study, I understand the seven trumpets will last 1,264 days and the seven bowls will last 70 days.

It was customary in ancient times for kings to destroy two thirds of the people who rebelled against them.[1] Kings did this because first, survivors could pay taxes and every king knew that more revenue in the treasury meant more money for his army. Second, if a conquered city was not destroyed, it became another outpost for the king. He did not have to spend time and resources to build a fort. Finally, the merciful act of sparing one third of the people quickly changed the loyalty of many survivors. The king was no longer viewed as an enemy, he was regarded a generous benefactor.

You need to understand this custom to appreciate the language used in the seven trumpets. In the following texts, notice the use of "thirds." God repetitively destroys one third, the inference, of course, is that He spares two thirds. This reveals God's great mercy for the people on Earth without using the word "mercy." Truth and gems have this element in common; they rarely lie on the surface.

First Trumpet: "A *third* of the earth was burned up, a *third* of the trees were burned up, and all the green grass was burned up."[2]

Second Trumpet: "A *third* of the sea turned into blood, a *third* of the living creatures in the sea died, and a *third* of the ships were destroyed."[3]

Third Trumpet: "A great star, blazing like a torch, fell from the sky on a *third* of the rivers and on the springs of water – the name

1   2 Samuel 8:1-2; Ezekiel 5:8-12; Zechariah 13:8
2   Revelation 8:7
3   Revelation 8:8-9

of the star is Wormwood. A *third* of the waters turned bitter, and many people died from the waters that had become bitter."[1]

Fourth Trumpet: "The fourth angel sounded his trumpet, and a *third* of the sun was struck, a *third* of the moon, and a *third* of the stars, so that a *third* of them turned dark. A *third* of the day was without light, and also a *third* of the night."[2]

Sixth Trumpet: "And the four angels who had been kept ready for this very hour and day and month and year were released to kill a *third* of mankind."[3]

I have called your attention to God's great mercy during the Great Tribulation to suggest that God may hold back the Antichrist for two thirds of the time allotted for the Great Tribulation. Daniel 12:11-12 indicates the Great Tribulation will last 1,335 days. This odd number of days is evenly divisible by thirds (1,335 days divided by 3 = 445 days). Therefore, if God mercifully keeps the devil in the Abyss for two thirds of the Great Tribulation, the devil would appear on the 891st day!

Beginning with Day One, the 144,000 servants of God would have about 29 months to present the gospel of Jesus before the Antichrist appears. This would be enough time for the world to hear and thoughtfully consider God's truth. This would also give time for a worldwide rebellion to occur. After the 144,000 have proclaimed the testimony of Jesus for 29 months to billions of people under the worst possible circumstances, most of the world's people will have decided to obey or reject the gospel of Jesus. If this scenario is true, the forward advance of the gospel ends as "the proper time" arrives for releasing the devil and his angels from the Abyss. The devil and his demons would be physically visible and active on Earth during the last one third (445 days) of the Great Tribulation.

The last three trumpets are called "woes" because they incorporate three curses poured upon wicked people. If God keeps the devil

---

1   Revelation 8:10-11
2   Revelation 8:12
3   Revelation 9:15

in the Abyss until the last third of the time allotted for the Great Tribulation, there is perfect harmony with the sum of the parts. After patiently waiting for 890 days for the people of Earth to hear the gospel and choose whom they will serve, God releases a destroyer (the Antichrist) to close the drama with sin and rebellion. If this scenario occurs, the final 445 days of Earth's history will be filled with unspeakable misery and suffering. Of course, time will tell.

No Judgments for Two Years

After the fourth judgment occurs, there likely will be no more judgments for over two years. Remember, I think the fifth trumpet could occur around the 890th day. Jesus holds the devil in the Abyss for two thirds of the 1,335 days allotted to the Great Tribulation. If my reasoning is correct, the religious leaders will boast that the apparent cessation of God's judgments for the two years proves their decision to create a worldwide church-state was God's will. Additionally, they will boast that their laws and punishments have been rewarded because no more judgments have fallen! Of course, this will be foolishness.

By the end of the fourth trumpet, the religious and political leaders of the world will have blasphemed God by condemning the "testimony of Jesus" given by the 144,000 true servant/prophets. Also, they will have inflicted much needless and bitter pain on people already hurting from God's judgments. Unforgivably, their stiff penalties have kept many people from embracing the gospel of Jesus. Many people do not have much faith in God during the good times, so when persecution is involved, suffering for Jesus makes cowards out of them. Notice what Jesus said, **"But the cowardly, the unbelieving, the vile, the murderers, the sexually immoral, those who practice magic arts, the idolaters and all liars – they will be confined to the fiery lake of burning sulfur. This is the second death."**[1] Jesus gave up everything to save repentant sinners and requires the same of His disciples. **"Anyone who loves their father or mother more than me is not worthy of me; anyone**

1 Revelation 21:8

who loves their son or daughter more than me is not worthy of me. Whoever does not take up their cross and follow me is not worthy of me. Whoever finds their life will lose it, and whoever loses their life for my sake will find it."[1]

Fifth Trumpet Explained

The Bible teaches God will release the devil and his demons at the fifth trumpet. God used ideas and objects in the vision from John's day that he understood. God wanted him to describe a scenario that has no equal or parallel in Earth's history, so God used "building blocks" familiar to John. Notice God's constant use of metaphors in the following texts to describe the prophecy by using familiar elements that John had seen or experienced. The scenario presented in the fifth trumpet makes sense once you understand the use of metaphors!

1. **"The fifth angel** [that stands before God] **sounded his trumpet, and I saw a star that had fallen from the sky to the earth."**[2] The fallen star is Satan, the *morning star, son of the dawn,* according to Isaiah 14:12 who was cast out of heaven because of his rebellion. The Lord said of Satan, **"Your heart became proud on account of your beauty, and you corrupted your wisdom because of your splendor. So I threw you to the earth."**[3] Centuries later, Jesus told His disciples, **"I saw Satan fall like lightning from heaven."**[4]

2. **"The star was given the key to the shaft of the Abyss."**[5] This sentence means that Satan cannot possibly escape the Abyss (the spirit realm) until God grants permission (gives him the key). Paul wrote, **"And now you know what is holding him** [the man of lawlessness] **back, so that he may be revealed at the proper time."**[6]

---

1   Matthew 10:37-39
2   Revelation 9:1, insertion mine
3   Ezekiel 28:17
4   Luke 10:18
5   Revelation 9:1
6   2 Thessalonians 2:6, insertion mine

3. **"When he [Satan] opened the Abyss, smoke rose from it like the smoke from a gigantic furnace. The *sun and sky* were darkened by the smoke from the Abyss. And out of the smoke *locusts came down* on the earth and were given power like that of scorpions of the earth."**[1] When the devil and his angels are released from the spirit realm, the world will be plagued by a swarm of demons physically descending from the sky! From John's perspective, the horde was so great he compared it to a dense swarm of locusts! Satan will descend from the sky masquerading as almighty God with millions of fallen angels obeying his commands.

The devil and his demons will imitate the Second Coming (descending from the sky) many times in order for people in different parts of the world to see their glory and power. They will walk on the earth, speaking and associating with people. This is unlike Jesus when He returns. Jesus will not touch the earth at the Second Coming. Instead, the saints will meet the Lord in the air.[2] Jesus will gather up the saints from Earth and take them to heaven to fulfill His promise.[3] Satan will have to walk and live on Earth to do accomplish his diabolical plans. He will promise one thousand years of peace and prosperity, but this is a lie. Jesus and the saints will not walk on the earth again until He creates a new heaven and Earth. The saints will reign with Jesus in heaven as judges during the one thousand years. Together, they will determine the amount of restitution wicked people suffer in hell.[4]

4. **"They [the demons] were told not to harm the grass of the earth or any plant or tree** [the devil and his angels are not permitted to destroy the earth during the five months of the fifth trumpet]**, but** [they are permitted to torture] **only those people who did not have the seal of God on their foreheads. They**

1   Revelation 9:2-3, insertion and italics mine
2   1 Thessalonians 4:16-17
3   John 14:2-3
4   1 Corinthians 6:2-3

were not allowed to kill them, but only to torture them for five months. And the agony they suffered was like that of the sting of a scorpion when it strikes. During those days people will seek death, but will not find it; they will long to die, but death will elude them."[1]

The devil and his demons will not be permitted to torture those who have the seal of God on their foreheads (the saints) during the five months of the fifth trumpet. The seal of God is a topic that everyone should study. (*wake-up.org/studies*) Briefly, the sealing points to an incredible gift which God will give to everyone who passes the test of faith. The first people to be sealed will be the 144,000. During the Great Tribulation, all who love the truth and pass the test of faith will also be "sealed." The sealing is the removal of the sinful nature and once the sinful nature is removed, a person will have no further inclination to sin!

When a person is born again, two natures constantly war against each other. The flesh wants one thing, the Spirit wants another. **"For if you live according to the flesh, you will die; but if by the Spirit you put to death the misdeeds of the body, you will live."**[2] When a person is sealed during the Great Tribulation, the desires of the sinful nature are removed and the door to temptation is closed! Individuals who receive the seal of God will be like Adam and Eve before they sinned!

During the fifth trumpet, the world will be divided into three groups of people. The first group, the saints, will be sealed after their test. I call the other two groups "the religious wicked" and "the nonreligious wicked." The religious wicked group is like the Pharisees when Jesus was on Earth. This group will be comprised of people who worship their religion because their religion is their god. These people do not love truth. They will reject the clearest evidence of God's will because they love their religion. These wicked people will easily fall for the devil's deceptions and

1   Revelation 9:4-6
2   Romans 8:13

after they see his miracles, they will believe that he is "God." The final group, the nonreligious wicked, is comprised of groups like communists, agnostics, and atheists. This is the group Satan's demons will attack and torture during the fifth trumpet.

The devil will not attack his followers and he cannot attack the saints, so his prey will be the remaining group, the nonreligious wicked. God restricts the devil because, at the end of the Great Tribulation, there will be two groups, sheep and goats. Everyone will either obey Jesus or the Antichrist. *"All* **inhabitants of the earth will worship the beast –** *all* **whose names have not been written in the Lamb's book of life, the Lamb who was slain from the creation of the world."**[1]

When the religious wicked and nonreligious wicked see the cruel torture Satan's angels inflict, God knows some individuals will reconsider the truth spoken by the 144,000 and repent of their rebellion. God wants to save everyone. He is not willing that any should perish, but He has no grace for rebellious people who defy His sovereign authority! Therefore, God allows the devil to do what he delights (torture people), so many religious and nonreligious people will come to their senses and realize that man is not sovereign. Instead, there is a higher power to which man must give an account. At the end of the Great Tribulation, everyone will be found obeying a higher power. Fortunately, during the time allotted for the seven trumpets, the door to salvation is still open.

5. **"The locusts looked like horses prepared for battle."**[2] John used the metaphor, *the locusts looked like,* so we can understand the demons are on a deadly mission. They will appear glorious and to those embracing the Antichrist as "God," they will pretend to be gracious to make Satan's deceit effective. Make no mistake, the demons are determined to destroy the human race and the world.

---

1   Revelation 13:8, italics mine
2   Revelation 9:7

"On their heads they wore something like crowns of gold, and their faces resembled human faces."[1] The metaphor, *crowns of gold,* means even the lowliest demon has sovereign authority over human beings. They have faces like human beings, because they were created in the image of God.

"Their hair was like women's hair, and their teeth were like lions' teeth."[2] The metaphor, *women's hair,* means they will be beautiful beings to look upon. Paul wrote, "If a woman has long hair, it is her glory? For long hair is given to her as a covering."[3] The metaphor, *lions' teeth,* means these aliens from the Abyss will be powerful and deadly. They will do whatever they want and mankind will be powerless to stop them. If the man of lawlessness has no respect for laws, and the religions and governments of the world, do you think his demons will be any different?

6. "They had breastplates like breastplates of iron, and the sound of their wings was like the thundering of many horses and chariots rushing into battle."[4] The metaphor, *breastplates of iron,* means they cannot be killed. The metaphor, *thundering of many horses and chariots,* means the whole world is under siege.

"They had tails with stingers like scorpions, and in their tails they had power to torment people for five months."[5] The metaphor, *like scorpions,* means they will be able to inflict searing pain on their helpless victims by simply touching them. When the five months have ended, many will remain among the nonreligious wicked group. The devil will kill them along with many others when the sixth trumpet occurs.

7. "They [the demons] had as king over them the angel of the Abyss, whose name in Hebrew is Abaddon and in Greek, is Apollyon (that is, Destroyer). The first woe [curse (fifth

1   Revelation 9:7
2   Revelation 9:8
3   1 Corinthians 11:15
4   Revelation 9:9
5   Revelation 9:10

trumpet)] **is past; two other woes** [two remaining curses] **are yet to come.**[1] The angel king of the Abyss is the devil, the man of lawlessness, the great red dragon, the beast that will come up from the Abyss and astonish the wicked. The two remaining curses are the sixth trumpet (second woe) and seventh trumpet (the third woe which marks the beginning of the seven bowls).

Satan's Worldwide Deceptions

The devil is the best Bible student on Earth. He maliciously uses his vast knowledge to diminish all that Jesus is and to keep people divided and confused. The devil was in the Garden of Eden when he spoke with Eve. He was in the camp when Moses descended Mt. Sinai with the Ten Commandments. He was in the city when Jericho fell, and he watched as Solomon dedicated the temple. He was present when Jesus went to the cross, and he was in the Roman prison when Paul was beheaded. The devil and his demons have attended every event in the Bible. Now that the Bible has exposed his identity, we can expect the devil to promote numerous lies about himself—the Antichrist! He is the father of lies and does not want anyone to hear or believe the truth.

John says in Revelation 9:5 that when the devil and his demons appear they will be given five months to deceive the world. Knowing they can teleport themselves and do not need sleep, it is easy to understand the devil and his demons will be constantly circling the globe performing miraculous acts. Jesus warned **"So if anyone tells you, 'There he is, out in the wilderness,' do not go out; or, 'Here he is, in the inner rooms,' do not believe it."**[2] The devil and his demons will make efficient use of the time by focusing on two groups of people: the religious wicked and nonreligious wicked.

The devil and his demons will concentrate on the religious wicked. This group will be easier to deceive since they already believe that God exists. When they see the devil's glory and his incredible

---

1   Revelation 9:11-12, insertions mine
2   Matthew 24:26

miracles, including his astonishing ability to call fire down from heaven, the religious wicked will believe his lies and worship him as almighty God. As he heals the sick and feeds thousands of starving people by multiplying a few sack lunches, the religious wicked will be eating out of his hand.

The devil is no fool. God's wrath is going to cause the world to be in a hopeless state. The devil will speak words of hope convincing people he has come to rebuild the world and establish the kingdom of God with one thousand years of peace and prosperity. Millions who are suffering will believe him and pin their hopes on this false prophet. I envision the devil's demons leading people in songs of praise and adoration. The overriding anthem will be "Holy, holy, holy, God lives among men!" Endless repetition of this phrase will have a mesmerizing effect.

Meanwhile, many of the devil's demons will be making house calls to find people in the nonreligious group. This group denies that God lives among men, or that God even exists! If reason does not prevail, the demons will use torture. Dictators know that when extremely painful torture is imposed on mom, dad, grandma, or grandpa, the remaining family members almost always will acquiesce to end the torture. Thus, many defiant and stubborn people will submit to the demands of the demons, worshiping and obeying the devil.

When the five months of the fifth trumpet are over, the sixth trumpet sounds. At this exact time to the very hour, which God set long ago, Jesus grants the devil permission to kill one third of mankind. The devil would kill everyone if permitted, but Jesus only grants him one third. When this moment occurs, the devil immediately discards the gracious and benevolent mask worn for five months. He and his demons have been planning for the sixth trumpet events for two thousand years. They have carefully planned their atrocities, and they have waited patiently until free to execute their plans.

When the devil and his demons are given power over life and death, there is nothing mankind can do to prevent their murderous plan. The

Man of Lawlessness is a fitting title because he will be a ruthless and cruel dictator. He will abolish the religions and governments of the world to set up his own one-world church-state. If God lives among men, how can a religion exist that opposes obedience to him? How can a government exist that opposes his will? No one can control or kill him. Those who are caught and refuse to worship the Antichrist will be put to death. Jesus will use the devil's desire to rule and ruin to still save souls!

Angels have far superior powers and abilities than mankind. When Jesus gives the Antichrist and his demons absolute power over the world, mankind will become their servants. When the devil asserts his authority, a great war will break out because, suddenly, the wicked will realize their loss of freedom. The devil's forces will kill one third of mankind in this war. This war will silence his opposition and establish the devil's undisputed rule over the world. Lucifer will become "king of kings" and "lord of lords" until Jesus appears. The Antichrist will do as he pleases; he will show no pity, no justice, and no tolerance. He will have no equal in history for committing crimes against humanity. If it were not for divine intervention, his evilness would destroy mankind completely.

God's Two Objectives

God is both deliberate and purposeful in everything He does. Before He does anything, He knows everything about the outcome. No unforeseen or unintended consequences surprise Him. One of the reasons Jesus releases the devil and his demons from the spirit realm at the fifth trumpet is because for 6,000 years, He has freely and generously allowed everyone on Earth to deny or believe in the existence of a "higher power." He has graciously allowed each person the free will to determine his own level of accountability to his God. This freedom will end when the Antichrist is released from the Abyss.

As I understand it, over a two-year period everyone will have a chance to hear the Creator's demands. The 144,000 will be speaking words from the Holy Spirit with penetrating power. They will exalt the Bible and use it to show their testimony is true; performing amazing miracles to confirm their testimony and ministry have divine credentials. Our Creator's will and demands will be as clear as He can make them. Nevertheless, after witnessing the horrific death and devastation caused by the first four judgments, much of the world will defy the gospel of Jesus revealed by the 144,000, Bible truth, and the Holy Spirit. Paul summarized this experience when he wrote, **"For that day** [the Second Coming] **will not come until the rebellion** *occ***urs and the man of lawlessness is revealed, the man doomed to destruction."**[1] **"They perish because they** [heard and] **refused to love the truth and so be saved. For this reason God sends them a powerful delusion so that they will believe the lie."**[2] Therefore, when the Antichrist is released at the fifth trumpet, Jesus will put the wicked on notice that everyone will submit to a higher power. It will be as though Jesus says, "You have a choice, pick one."

The release of the devil and his demons at the fifth trumpet initiates another interesting process. Jesus wants to save every sinner. However, to move the last few sinners past their rebellion, Jesus releases the devil and his demons. The devil knows his punishment cannot be pardoned. He also understands the book of Revelation and knows his fate. Jesus understands the devil is eager to "rule and ruin" the earth. He knows the devil has wanted to be worshiped as God for thousands of years. Jesus also knows the devil is eager to torture and destroy mankind. Satan hates Jesus and the Father with a passion that goes beyond man's comprehension.

Jesus knows the devil's desires. When the 144,000 and Holy Spirit's work stalls because billions of people are unwilling to obey His gospel, Jesus will release Satan and give him power over mankind. If Jesus allows the devil to deceive the religious wicked and torture the nonreligious wicked, it is because He knows some wicked people in each group will wake up, repent, and choose salvation!

---

1   2 Thessalonians 2:3, insertion mine
2   2 Thessalonians 2:10-11, insertion mine

This choice will prove far better than submitting to the authority of the abominable Antichrist! Jesus knows that giving a fatally ruined Earth over to the devil to "rule and ruin" in exchange for a few souls is a great deal for both parties!

Seven Religious Systems

The book of Revelation divides the people of the world into seven general religious systems: Atheism (agnostics, deists, etc.), Heathenism (tribal religions, occult groups such as Wiccan, etc.), Judaism (Orthodox, Reformed, etc.), Islam (Sunni, Shiite, etc.), Eastern Mysticism (Hinduism, Buddhism, etc.), Catholicism (Orthodox, Greek, Anglican, etc.), and Protestantism (Baptists, Pentecostals, etc.). The Bible considers Atheism to be a religion because like the other systems, it is a faith-based belief system. Atheists believe there is no God.

When Jesus selects the 144,000, He will choose unlikely individuals for the position. Each one will personally meet with Jesus. Once Jesus explains His presence, they will immediately recognize and worship Him as their Creator and Savior! Jesus will give each one the words they are to speak, represented as a little book in Ezekiel 3 and Revelation 10. The 144,000 will stand firm in their faith because they will be sealed with Holy Spirit power. They will come from every tongue, culture, and religious background. Because Jesus wants to save as many people as possible, He will select and empower those who can best represent Him before their own people.

Jesus understands man's religious bias, cultural prejudice, and ethnic suspicion. Remember, Jesus did live on Earth for a while. Currently, a Muslim cannot tell a Protestant that the Protestant faith is false and expect a pleasant outcome. Likewise, a Catholic cannot tell a Jew his religion is false and expect an endearing response. However, an enlightened Catholic can speak to his Catholic brothers and sisters, an enlightened Muslim can speak to his Muslim brothers and sisters, an enlightened Jew can speak to Jews, and an enlightened Protestant can speak to Protestants (maybe)!

Three Convenient Lies

The devastation caused by the four judgments described in Revelation 8 will cause religious and political leaders of the world to quickly assemble to discuss God's wrath. World leaders will set aside religious and political differences due to the fear of God because their respective nations will be in ruins and two billion people will be missing, dead, or dying. Seeing the calamity and fearing more imminent displays of God's wrath, leaders of the world will discuss inflammatory topics behind closed doors.

Religious leaders of the world will be unable to resolve their religious conflicts. However, they know billions of terrified people are anxious for an explanation and solution to stop God's wrath. The clergy will agree on an astonishing solution and political leaders will have little choice but to accept. They will acknowledge something must be done or God will soon destroy the world! Given the fear and extremity of the moment, religious leaders will compromise on certain fundamental beliefs thereby appearing united. These convenient lies are needed to justify their plan to save planet Earth from further acts of God.

I call these "convenient lies" because they will not be a malicious or a deliberate effort to mislead people. Given the dire circumstances, these lies will be the best that world leaders can do. They will be convenient in the sense they are both expedient and somewhat reasonable. The clergy will assume most of their constituency will comply. The greatest lie is they can presume to appease God's wrath. This proves that they do not know God and His Word, character, ways, or plans; but profess to. Additionally, the clergy will not realize it at the time, but their convenient lies will be their undoing when the devil and his demons appear at the fifth trumpet.

The First Lie

The first question on every survivor's mind will be "Who is doing this? Who is angry? Is it the Muslim god, Allah; the Jewish God,

Jehovah; the Christian God called the Father; or the Hindu God, Shiva?" Of course, no one will be able to definitively answer the question. This will lead to another provocative and potentially inflammatory question: "Does mankind worship one God having different titles or many different gods?"

How can this be when Jews worship Jehovah, the God of Abraham, Isaac, and Jacob; but Muslims worship Allah, the God of Abraham, Ishmael, and Mohammed. If Jews and Muslims worship the same God, why is God's will for Jews different from the teachings of Mohammed? The Bible exalts Jacob's descendants, not Ishmael's descendants.[1] The Book of Islam exalts Mohammed as a prophet and excludes the testimony of Old Testament prophets. If Jehovah and Allah are titles for the same God, why does a great antagonistic gulf exist between the two religions?

To make matters worse, the gods of Muslims, Jews, and Hindus do not have a son called Jesus and these religious systems strenuously oppose the idea that Jesus is deity—the Creator of the world. If Jesus is deity, He is greater than Mohammed and that is not a possibility for Muslims. Likewise, Catholics and Protestants have conflicts. Both religious systems believe in "The Father, Son, and Holy Ghost" but they are far apart on what constitutes "The Father, Son, and Holy Ghost" as well as the process of salvation.

Even though everyone agrees there is an angry God, how does a religiously and politically diverse world worship and appease whichever god has devastated the world and killed two billion people? Consider the problems these questions will create.

So the first lie will be that everyone on Earth worships the same God, even though we worship Him in different ways and call Him by different names and titles. Billions of people will accept this lie, because they do not understand enough about God and/or other religions to know the truth. Since it is politically and religiously inflammatory to declare anyone's god a false god, this lie will be a

---

1   Genesis 17:18-21

convenient way to get around the question of which god is angry. Furthermore, survivors will be so traumatized that most of them will not care. They will go along, to get along, with whatever the experts say because they just want God's wrath to end!

The first lie will give survivors a sense of community because all humanity must work together to appease God. However, the first lie will produce an inflammatory conflict. The 144,000 will tell the world that Jesus rules on heaven's throne as almighty God and it was He who sent the judgments.[1]

Jesus will tell the world through the 144,000 that He is Creator and judge of mankind, and He is returning soon to save those who will repent of their sins, put their faith in Him, and obey His gospel. The 144,000 will also declare that when Jesus returns, He will destroy His enemies. Of course, during the early days of the Great Tribulation, people will not realize that it is actually Jesus speaking through the 144,000. Their experience will be identical to God's prophets in Bible times when most were killed for speaking Jesus' words which were considered offensive.[2]

The Second Lie

Religious leaders will advocate a second lie to appease God. They will claim God's wrath fell on notably wicked places in every nation which proves all nations and peoples are accountable to Him. Clearly, God has been offended and is angry with our sinful and decadent ways. They will say that to appease God's wrath, we must worship Him, repent and change. We cannot turn a blind eye and ignore any behavior that is offensive to God. Although their claim will seem reasonable, it will be false. If the religious leaders of the world properly understood the books of Daniel and Revelation, they would have anticipated God's wrath and known His purposes for the judgments. They would also know that appeasing Jesus is not an option. Nothing can stop the seven

---

1   Ephesians 1:9-10; Daniel 7:13-14; Revelation 19:16
2   Matthew 23:37

trumpets. Jesus will close the drama with sin by separating the sheep from the goats.

The first four trumpets will be followed by the fifth! To appease God's wrath, the religious and political leaders of the world will create a monstrosity of a government: the seven-headed beast described in Revelation 13:1-8. This beast will be a worldwide church-state, governed by seven religious dictators from the seven religious systems of the world. Religious leaders will dictate the rules, political leaders will implement their demands, and law enforcement personnel will ensure compliance. Anyone who refuses will be severely punished.

The clergy will assume that God's wrath has broken out because the world is too corrupt and evil, and if corruption and evil are eliminated, God's favor will return. They will attempt to do this by creating a long list of sinless laws and severely punishing offenders. God knows that man's sinful nature is his greatest problem and coerced conduct does not change man's heart. God wants freewill beings! He wants a person, of his own free will, to consider God's love and His offer of salvation. If that person is moved by the Holy Spirit to obey the gospel of Jesus and becomes a repentant sinner, this pleases God and makes salvation possible!

The upcoming crisis government has seven heads because there are seven religious systems. Each religious system will have its own dictator. This beast of a government will try to appease God according to seven different versions of what is believed to please Him. This will be impossibly stupid. The clergy agreed to the convenient lie that there is one God; however, each head will go about representing God as though there were seven Gods! All seven heads will blaspheme (insult) God! This is why a blasphemous name is written on each of their heads![1] Man's response to God's judgments will be a horrible case of the "blind leading the blind."[2] The Bible predicts the whole world will

---

1   Revelation 13:1
2   Matthew 15:14

follow the seven-headed beast as it leads the way into greater misery and blasphemy![1]

The Third Lie

The leaders of the seven-headed beast will create a third convenient lie to justify their extreme solution to appease God. This lie will be that the creation of a worldwide religious authority [seven-headed beast] is God's will. They will claim to have created the government which provides divine direction for all nations. The political leaders of the world will then enforce the laws deemed necessary to rid the world of evil to appease God. Repentance and reformation will be mandatory if people want to, once again, enjoy God's favor and blessings.

The clergy will quickly conclude global reformation is only possible if all political leaders give them unfettered authority to accomplish their objectives. Since martial law will be in effect around the world, constitutional and legislative protection for human rights will not interfere with the clergy's unrestrained and insane overreach. Remember, the clergy will be terrified of God's wrath like everyone else. This is exactly what the devil wants.

Even though the devil and demons will be in the Abyss until the fifth trumpet, Satan will have a huge role in the formation and power of the seven-headed beast. The Bible says, **"The dragon** [the devil] **gave the** [seven-headed] **beast his power and his throne and great authority."**[2] Make no mistake about this: Even though the devil has been confined to the Abyss for thousands of years, his work and influence around the world is tremendous! The devil and his demons control many people. The devil has enormous influence within the seven religious systems of the world! The devil will give miracle-working powers to certain people to confirm that the creation of the seven-headed beast is God's will![3] Their astonishing miracles will convince the world's political leaders that God is demanding

1   Revelation 13:3
2   Revelation 13:2, insertions mine
3   Matthew 7:21-22

dramatic change. Jesus warned, **"For false messiahs and false prophets will appear and perform great signs and wonders to deceive, if possible, even the elect. See, I have told you ahead of time."**[1]

Antichrist Uses the Three Lies

We have considered the identity of the Antichrist, when he will appear, and God's first four judgments resulting in the formation of the seven-headed beast. The Antichrist is a master of manipulation and the father of lies. He will use the three convenient lies to manipulate the religious leaders of the world to facilitate his future agenda. Notice how each lie will fit into the devil's masquerade when Jesus allows him to appear.

Lie #1: Everyone on Earth worships the same God, even though we worship Him in different ways and call Him by different names and titles.

The Antichrist will use this lie to give himself immediate credibility. He will say words to the effect, "In times past, I was worshiped according to various titles created by different religions, but this practice ends today. I am God. There is no other." Paul wrote, **"[H]e sets himself up in God's temple, proclaiming himself to be God. He** [the Man of Lawlessness] **will use all sorts of displays of power through signs and wonders that serve the lie** [that he is God]**, and all the ways that wickedness deceives those who are perishing."**[2]

John wrote, **"And it** [the beast that rises from the Abyss, which is the Antichrist, the devil] **performed great signs, even causing fire to come down from heaven to the earth in full view of the people. Because of the signs it was given power** [from God] **to perform on behalf of the first beast, it**[, the beast, the devil,] **deceived the inhabitants of the earth** [with his lies and miracles]**."**[3] During the five months of the fifth trumpet, the devil will appear to honor and

---

1   Matthew 24:24-25
2   2 Thessalonians 2:4, 9-10, insertions mine
3   Revelation 13:13-14, insertions mine

exalt the church/state (seven-headed beast) created by the clergy. Later, he will turn it into a great advantage at the sixth trumpet.

The seven-headed beast will pursue and relentlessly persecute the saints. John wrote, **"It** [the seven-headed beast, the crisis-government, the religious authority directing the appeasement of God] **was given power to wage war against God's holy people and to conquer them. And it was given authority over every tribe, people, language and nation** [without firing a single bullet].**"**[1] **"The beast** [the seven-headed beast] **was given a mouth to utter proud words and blasphemies and to exercise its authority for forty-two months."**[2]

When the devil appears at the fifth trumpet, he will proclaim the greatness of the seven-headed beast and honor the world's religious leaders for punishing those who refused to obey its laws. Of course, the clergy will gladly receive "God's" praise; but Jesus warned His disciples, **"In fact, the time is coming when anyone who kills you will think they are offering a service to God. They will do such things because they have not known the Father or me."**[3]

For five months, the devil will be on a determined mission to convince the entire world he is God. Building on the clergy's lie, he will proclaim himself to be the one and only God. Daniel wrote, **"The** [fierce-looking] **king will do as he pleases. He will exalt and magnify himself above every god and will say unheard-of things against the God of gods. He will be successful until the time of wrath is completed, for what has been determined must take place."**[4]

Satan will claim since he has arrived to establish the kingdom of God on Earth, everyone must abandon his former religious beliefs and embrace the truth about God. Paul wrote, **"He will oppose and will exalt himself over everything that is called God or is worshiped,**

1   Revelation 13:7, insertions mine
2   Revelation 13:5, insertion mine
3   John 16:2-3
4   Daniel 11:36, insertion mine

so that he sets himself up in God's temple, proclaiming himself to be God."[1]

It is very important to understand that the devil will oppose everything having to do with God. This means he will not favor Muslims over Catholics, or Hindus over Jews. He will be equally opposed to Protestants and Atheists. If the devil were to show favoritism for one religious group, he would alienate the other groups and ruin his objective to make the entire world worship him as God. Because of man's natural bias toward the religious system with which he is most familiar, a Protestant would not worship the Antichrist who advocates Islam. Likewise, a Muslim would not worship the Antichrist who advocates Judaism. Paul's words must be strongly considered to avoid being deceived by the Antichrist!

The lie that mankind worships one God who is called by different names will play directly into the devil's coming deception. Be prepared. To show his disregard for the religions of the world, Satan will even establish a new day for worship!

Lie #2: We must worship God, repent, and change to appease His wrath.

During the five months the devil is deceiving the world, he will claim that he withheld his wrath for two years because of the sincere and excellent work of the religious and political leaders. Their dedication has been rewarded with no further judgments. He will commend them for severely punishing the rebels (actually, the saints). The devil will appear to be gracious and benevolent, but he will remind his audiences that to avoid further judgments, a deeper repentance and more substantial changes are required now that God lives among men! A new era has begun and it requires a new mindset.

The devil will use Lie #2 many times to prepare unsuspecting people for the abrupt changes he will force on them as soon as the five months of the fifth trumpet have ended. Jesus prevents the devil from killing a large portion of mankind for five months because He

1   2 Thessalonians 2:4

has higher power and objectives. Jesus wants to save defiant people from the devil's clutches if at all possible.

As the devil's popularity grows around the world, he will begin to teach that all religious requirements must change. "Now that God lives among us, there must be one Lord, one faith and one baptism! How can it be otherwise? Believe in me; put your trust in me; worship me! I have come to establish the kingdom of God on Earth for the next one thousand years. I have to purge the earth of unbelievers to do this! Do not harden your heart! Change your mind and let your past religious beliefs go. Give God your loyal affection. Change your ways and do as I command you, and you will be blessed starting today!" After seeing more signs and wonders and listening to his gentle persuasion (remember, he deceived one third of the angels in heaven), this master of lies will seduce multitudes of people.

Lie #3: The creation of a worldwide religious authority (seven-headed beast) is God's will.

Jesus will give the devil absolute power over Earth with permission to kill one third of mankind at the sixth trumpet. When the devil receives this power, he will cause an unimaginable uproar throughout Earth.

The devil will say words to this effect, "The formation of a worldwide church-state, governed by seven religious leaders has served well. You have heard me praise your leaders for all that they have accomplished. Millions of rebellious and defiant people have been punished for disobedience. However, now that I have come to establish the kingdom of God on Earth for the next one thousand years, a similar, but much better, form of government is needed so that everyone will have one king, one lord, one faith, and one baptism. Therefore, I am declaring myself king of Earth and the kingdom of God will be established among men. The religions and governments of the world are hereby abolished. I will declare the laws of the kingdom. All who refuse to obey and worship me will be captured and killed. I must purge Earth of rebellion! The earlier laws (from the seven-headed beast) must give way to my theocracy. I will rule as Lord of lords and King of kings and be worshiped as almighty God. The penalty for defiance is death."

John wrote, **"It** [the beast from the Abyss, the devil] **ordered them** [the people of the world] **to set up an image** [a clone or mirror of the church-state created by religious leaders] **in honor of the** [seven-headed] **beast who** [had a head that] **was wounded by the sword and yet lived. The second beast** [the beast from the Abyss] **was given power** [from God] **to give breath** [life] **to the image** [the mirror] **of the first beast** [the clone which the devil demands will be a theocracy]**, so that the image** [the devil's clone] **could speak** [make laws] **and cause all who refused to worship** [obey] **the image** [his theocracy] **to be killed** [because the beast from the Abyss has been given absolute power over mankind]**."**[1]

The religious and political leaders of the world will be shocked! For five months "God" has been praising their efforts to appease his wrath by punishing the saints; but now, he throws them under the bus and counts anyone who resists as worthy of death! This is the way the devil works. He uses flattery, deception, and lies to obtain whatever he wants. He loves and appreciates no one. The religious and political leaders of the world will unite to stop his tyranny, but it will be a losing battle. This coming world war is described in Revelation 9:13-21.

Jesus is Revealed

The titles, "man of lawlessness," "great red dragon," "Satan," "beast from the Abyss," "false prophet," "angel king of the Abyss," "Abaddon and Apollyon," and "son of the dawn" are assigned to the devil and describe dimensions of his character and activity. The Bible uses the same application for Jesus. Titles for Him include, "Lamb of God," "Son of God," "Son of Man," "Holy One," "Messiah," and "Word of God." Each title adds an important dimension to enhance

---

1   Revelation 13:14-15, insertions mine

our understanding of Jesus. Students of the Bible need to carefully consider each dimension to understand the person being studied.

I have mentioned titles for Jesus and the devil because the title "Antichrist" may be misleading. The Antichrist will not imitate the Christ most Christians perceive. However, Satan will certainly imitate the Christ who currently rules over heaven and Earth as almighty God![1]

In 1798, Jesus was found worthy[2] to receive the Book of Life which was secured with seven seals. At that time, the Father recused Himself by giving Jesus His (the Father's) throne and sovereign power. Thus far, while ruling over heaven and Earth,[3] Jesus has broken the first three seals on the Book of Life. The Father gave His throne and sovereign power to Jesus because the Father wants the universe to understand Jesus is also a God now living in human form. By stepping aside, the Father wants everyone to know that Jesus is as powerful and capable of running the universe. They are self-existing Gods; this means both Gods have no beginning or end. They were together in the beginning before anything existed and their relationship will never end. When the Father gave His throne to Jesus in 1798, the "revelation of Jesus Christ" began. This will conclude at the end of the 1,000 years after everyone in the universe learns Jesus is almighty God like the Father.

After the revelation of Jesus is completed, He will return to the Father the throne and sovereign power received in 1798. Paul says, **"Then the end will come, when he [Jesus] hands over the kingdom to God the Father after he [Jesus] has destroyed all dominion, authority and power [on Earth]. For he [Jesus] must reign [on the throne] until he [Jesus] has put all his enemies under his feet. The last enemy to be destroyed is death. For he [the** Father] 'has put everything under his [Jesus'] feet.' Now when it says that 'everything' has been put under him [Jesus], it is

---

1   Reference material posted at wake-up.org/studies
2   Revelation 5
3   Daniel 7:13-14; Ephesians 1:9-10

clear that this does not include God [the Father] **himself, who put everything under Christ.**[1] **When he** [Jesus] **has done this** [destroyed the curse of sin which produces death], **then the Son himself will** [once again] **be made subject to him** [the Father] **who put everything under him, so that God** [the Father] **may** [return to His throne and] **be all in all.**"[2]

Jesus was given the throne and sovereign power to bring the drama with sin to a close in a specific way that allows for no omissions or additions to complete the task associated with each seal on the Book of Life. Jesus, ruling as almighty God, will soon break the fourth seal and eight billion or more people will experience the divine authority and devastating power of a sovereign Jesus. He will send four judgments (the first four trumpets in Revelation 8:7-12) which will destroy most of Earth; two billion people will die. This coming apocalyptic horror will be devastating, but it will cause people to learn about Jesus' authority and divinity. Billions of non-Christians will be stunned when they learn that Jesus is almighty God having greater authority than the false gods of the world. Jesus is the Creator of heaven and Earth returning to gather His people and to destroy the governments and false religions of the world.

Meanwhile, millions of Christians who worship a Jesus that resembles "Santa Claus" rather than a king will become very bitter toward Him when they learn He is responsible for all the death and destruction caused by the first four trumpets. Although most Christians have a Bible, they do not search it for truth. Sadly, thousands of Christian clergy have created a mistaken perception of Jesus. There is much more to Jesus than one title can declare. Yes, He was a "man of sorrows,"[3] but He can also be a fierce king.[4] John describes Jesus at the Second Coming as an angry general, leading an army bent on conquest: **"Coming out of his mouth is a sharp sword with which to strike down the nations. 'He will rule them with an iron**

---

1   Ephesians 1:9-10
2   1 Corinthians 15:24-28, insertions mine
3   Isaiah 53:2-3
4   Psalm 2:12

scepter.' He treads the winepress of the fury of the wrath of God Almighty. On his robe and on his thigh he has this name written: King of Kings and Lord of Lords."[1]

Understand, the Father, the Son, and the Holy Spirit are three equal, distinct, self-existing Gods who love mercy as much as they love justice. All three Gods love righteousness as much as they hate evil. When Jesus breaks the fourth seal and releases fury and wrath, the Father, Son, and Holy Spirit will be in perfect agreement because they are one in purpose, plan, and action.

The devil will use Jesus' current position, as almighty God, for his masquerade. Remember, the Antichrist will imitate a Christ most people do not know! If the devil appeared claiming to be Jesus, what effect would he have on Atheists, Hindus, Buddhists, Muslims, and Jews? The devil knows he and his demons will have only five months at the fifth trumpet to deceive the whole world. He has to appear as almighty God to make his deception work. If he appeared claiming to be Jesus, he would alienate a large majority of the world! This is why Paul says the man of lawlessness will oppose all that is called God or is worshiped.

The Great Enlightenment

The "Great Tribulation" is a term Christians use to describe a future event which will be the most difficult period in Earth's history. The Father has embedded another great purpose within the Great Tribulation which is to enlighten the world about the revelation of Jesus. Only God's wrath could grasp the attention of a rebellious world mired in religious contempt and political gridlock.

After one third of the Earth is burned, thousands of cities destroyed, and global darkness causes famine, most survivors will recognize the authority of Jesus as almighty God. The world has seen His authority; now, the world needs to hear about the love Jesus has for sinners. The 144,000, with Holy Spirit power, will tell the world about Jesus. The 144,000 will proclaim his offer of salvation, but this enlightenment

1   Revelation 19:15-16

will cause many problems. The devil will persecute any person who receives Jesus as his Savior. Nevertheless, the whole world will be enlightened with the truth about Jesus. His gospel will separate the sheep from the goats as a magnet separates steel from aluminum.

When our Creator came to Earth as a baby, He came in obscurity. Only the wise men and some shepherds were aware of His birth. Even the religious leaders in Jerusalem did not know. Long ago, the Father ordained the return of our Creator would be entirely different. Jesus' next appearance on Earth will not be a friendly visit. Instead, He is returning to rescue and resurrect each repentant sinner and to destroy His enemies. For 1,260 days, the 144,000 will present the terms and conditions for salvation so individuals can intelligently decide whether to obey and worship Jesus as almighty God and inherit His coming kingdom.

Initially, most of the world will reject what they hear. The truth about Jesus and His coming kingdom will be contrary to the beliefs of Muslims, Hindus, Buddhists, Jews, Catholics, Protestants, Atheists, and Pagans! However, since two billion people have died from the horrific destruction caused by God's wrath, the extremity of these circumstances will subdue most people and provide them a chance to hear and consider Jesus' first message.

Timing is Crucial

Shortly before Jesus breaks the fourth seal on the Book of Life, He will select and empower 144,000 servants to speak for Him. If there are eight billion people living on Earth today and 25% are destroyed by God's wrath during the first four trumpets, six billion people will survive. If six billion people are equally served by 144,000 prophets, each servant of God will minister to approximately 42,000 people over the course of 1,260 days which represents about 34 per day. These estimates highlight two points.

First, because of God's love for all mankind, we can assume the 144,000 will be equally distributed around the world so each survivor hears the gospel of Jesus. If India has a population of 1.25 billion survivors after the first four trumpets, this indicates ~26,750 of the 144,000 will be serving in India! If the population of the United States is reduced to 270 million after the first four trumpets, about ~6,425 of the 144,000 will be serving this country.

Second, reaching 34 per day is not unreasonable when we consider the trauma and terror of the time. Initially, most survivors will have a great thirst for knowledge. Because communication infrastructures will be non- existent, little information will be available. However, God's servants will be in place and, empowered by the Holy Spirit, ready to proclaim the everlasting gospel on Day One! God's wrath will have the crucial effect of silencing mankind. Believers and nonbelievers will be speechless, giving God's messengers the opportunity to be heard. This is how the great enlightenment begins. Each kindred, tongue, and people will hear the "testimony of Jesus" as He speaks through the mouths of His servants.

If the severity of the first four trumpets is overwhelming, the great enlightenment that occurs will be no less traumatic. According to Revelation 7:9-17, the revelation of Jesus will cause the honest in heart to leave (exit, renounce, and abandon) their religious and political heritage. Jesus, reigning as almighty God, will speak His truth and decisions will be made. "When a man who is honestly mistaken hears the truth, he will either quit being mistaken or cease being honest." – Richard J. Humpal, Attorney. John saw a numberless multitude embrace Jesus as their King and Redeemer! Six billion people will hear four messages.

The First Message

The Holy Spirit will work through the 144,000 as He did through Jesus! Their miracles will affirm their divine appointment and mission.[1] The 144,000 will exalt the Bible which becomes the book of great importance as it is closely studied. The Bible will confirm their testimony is true! Jesus will give the 144,000 words to speak

---

1   See Acts 14:3 for a comparison.

when arguments against His truth are encountered.[1] This will be a replay of when Jesus was on Earth! As the Pharisees tried to trap Jesus with His own words, the Father instantly gave Jesus the words to speak! Jesus said, **"Don't you believe that I am in the Father, and that the Father is in me? The words I say to you I do not speak on my own authority. Rather, it is the Father, living in me, who is doing his work."[2] "For I did not speak on my own, but the Father who sent me commanded me to say all that I have spoken."[3]**

Before we examine the first message, please understand a basic fact: Jesus, not the Father, is the Creator of heaven and Earth. The Father designed them, but Jesus built them. Paul wrote, **"For in him [Jesus] all things were created: things in heaven and on earth, visible and invisible, whether thrones or powers or rulers or authorities; all things have been created through him and for him. He is before all things, and in him all things hold together."[4]**

Paul also wrote, **"In the past God [the Father] spoke to our ancestors through the prophets at many times and in various ways, but in these last days he has spoken to us by his Son, whom he appointed heir of all things, and through whom also he made the universe."[5]**

John wrote, **"Through him [Jesus] all things were made; without him nothing was made that has been made."[6] "He [Jesus] was in the world, and though the world was made through him, the world did not recognize him. He came to that which was his own, but his own [people] did not receive him."[7]**

Jesus is the Creator because the 144,000's first message during the great enlightenment period will come as a demand from Jesus.

---

1   Mark 13:11
2   John 14:10
3   John 12:49
4   Colossians 1:16-17, insertion mine
5   Hebrews 1:1-2, insertion mine
6   John 1:3, insertion mine
7   John 10-11, insertions mine

"Then I [John] **saw another angel flying in midair** [the angel's midair position indicates he has a message from God for the world below], **and he had the eternal gospel** [the eternal or everlasting gospel is a law which the Father put into effect before anything was created. This law existed long before sin occurred and it requires everyone to worship Jesus as they worship the Father[1] because Jesus is a God like the Father.[2] The divinity of Jesus is veiled in human form, but Jesus is much more than a human! John saw a messenger sent from heaven] **to proclaim** [this law] **to those who live on the earth – to every nation, tribe, language and people. He said in a loud voice, 'Fear God** [show great reverence and respect, be cautious and afraid of Jesus] **and give him glory** [by recognizing His authority and obeying His demands], **because the hour of his judgment has come** [Jesus will judge everyone[3]]. **Worship him** [as the everlasting gospel requires,] **who made the heavens, the earth** [the land], **the sea and the springs of water.'**"[4]

The last sentence mentions the heavens, Earth, sea, and springs of water. These are the elements our Creator will destroy with the first four trumpet/judgments! The first trumpet/judgment burns one third of Earth, the second destroys one third of the sea, the third poisons the water supply of a continent, and the fourth fills the heavens with darkness and debris. Therefore, the 144,000 will say "Give Him glory; revere and obey your Creator, He is almighty God! There is no God like Jesus! If you give Him glory, He will eagerly save you and grant you eternal life!"

This enlightenment will be inflammatory for three reasons.

1. Because the 144,000 will be selected from all religious systems, survivors from each system will be appalled to hear *one of their own* saying, "Jesus Christ is almighty God who will soon return to Earth. He has sent judgments to signal His displeasure with the wickedness of mankind. He is the Creator and must

---

1   John 5:22-23
2   John 1:1-2, 10, 18
3   2 Corinthians 5:10; Ecclesiastes 12:13-14
4   Revelation 14:6-7, insertions mine

be respected, revered, and worshiped on His holy day which is Saturday, the seventh day of the week!"

It will be one matter to hear that Jesus Christ is almighty God; it will be another to hear that Jesus commands everyone to keep holy His seventh day. These two topics will infuriate billions of people. If it were not for the devastating destruction, the loss of life, and the power of the Holy Spirit resting upon them, the 144,000 would be killed for these inflammatory declarations.

2. The 144,000 will also tell the inhabitants of Earth that Jesus is the judge of mankind and the time for judging the living has arrived. If any person wishes to have a part in the coming kingdom of God, he must put his faith in Jesus and obey the eternal gospel without regard for consequences. Additionally, all sinners must make conditions right with those they have wronged by providing restitution, if possible. Sinners must repent and forsake any unrighteous behavior before the end of mercy.

3. Another message the 144,000 will give is that Jesus is not returning for a visit. For those who choose to put their faith in Him, He comes as the *Lamb of God*. For those who choose to defy His everlasting gospel and gracious offer of salvation, He will appear as the *Lion from the tribe of Judah*. As our Creator, He is entitled to our loyalty and submission. He is the only Savior and wants to save every sinner. He loves us and gave His life for us so we could have salvation. Therefore, He says, "Do not harden your hearts. Receive Me as your King and Redeemer; I will gladly save you! I will call for you when I set up My kingdom and give you eternal life and endless happiness!"

Be aware of four conditions that will arise during the great enlightenment.

First, the Great Tribulation will be a time of great injustice for God's people. The devil has been preparing to make war on the saints since

1798! The Bible says: **"And the** [great red] **dragon was wroth** [became angry when Jesus brought Satan's control over Europe through the Catholic Church to an end in 1798, the devil was furious] **with the woman** [God's people], **and went** [off to prepare] **to make war with the remnant of her seed** [that is, the last generation of God's people[1]], **which keep the commandments of God** [including the fourth commandment], **and have the testimony of Jesus Christ** [among them, spoken through the mouths of the 144,000]."[2]

Second, the idea of creating a seven-headed beast to appease God's wrath will be a giant smoke screen. Like any statist government, the devil will facilitate the creation and empowerment of the seven-headed beast to obtain what he wants. **"The dragon gave the** [seven-headed] **beast his power and his throne and great authority."**[3] The devil is determined to establish the perception of appeasing God's wrath because he wants to destroy the remnant of God's people before Jesus arrives to rescue them!

Third, contemplate the following fact: **"It** [the seven-headed beast] **was given power to wage war against God's holy people and to conquer them. And it** [the seven-headed beast] **was given authority over every tribe, people, language and nation."**[4] Understand the devil's primary objective is to destroy God's people. The destruction of billions of people in two groups, the religious wicked and nonreligious wicked, is merely collateral damage. By depriving God's people of justice and persecuting them in every way possible, the devil plans to eliminate the saints before his allotted time expires.

Fourth, efforts of the devil to annihilate God's people will have a destructive effect but not the murderous result he wants. God will give His faith-full people courage, patience, and endurance to stand firm because salvation only comes through faith! The furnace of persecution will make their faith purer and stronger. They will be

1   Genesis 3:15
2   Revelation 12:17, KJV, insertions mine
3   Revelation 13:2, insertion mine
4   Revelation 13:7, insertions mine

more determined than ever to worship Jesus as the first message demands. A numberless multitude out of every religious system and government will be saved! **"After this I looked and there before me was a great multitude that no one could count, from every nation, tribe, people and language, standing before the throne and before the Lamb. They were wearing white robes and were holding palm branches in their hands."**[1] **"These are they** *who have come out of the great tribulation*; **they have washed their robes and made them white in the blood of the Lamb."**[2]

The Second Message

The monster of a government is described in Revelation 13:1-2 as a beast rising out of the sea, which represents the nations of the world, and resembles a leopard.[3] It will have seven heads and ten horns and wield the dreadful power of tyranny given it by the devil.

A brief description explains how the seven-headed beast rises. World leaders will assemble and conclude that God's wrath has fallen on mankind because of wickedness. Their solution is to eliminate all vice. The religious leaders will insist that a worldwide religious authority be established to eliminate global wickedness. This crisis-driven government will be tasked with the mandate to appease God and will be given power and authority to severely punish anyone who disobeys its laws. This religious authority (beast) will have seven governors (heads) because there are seven global religious systems. The Bible gives this beast the title, Babylon, because it will be a church/state like ancient Babylon.[4] This background is needed to understand the enlightenment that comes with the second message,

"A second angel followed [in midair] **and said** [to the inhabitants on Earth below], ' "Fallen! [false, corrupt, blasphemous] Fallen is Babylon the Great** [the seven-headed beast, Babylon, is an insult

---

1   Revelation 7:9
2   Revelation 7:14, italics mine
3   Revelation 17:15
4   Daniel 3

to Jesus. In its effort to appease God, it actually leads the world into defiance against the eternal gospel and Christ's demand to keep holy His Sabbath day! The clergy of the world will insist on worshiping God but not according to our Creator's demand! The beast]," **which made all the nations drink the maddening wine of her adulteries** [is drunk with arrogance and ignorance. Babylon defies God's Word and it is highly offensive to Jesus.]'"[1]

The phrase, "drink the maddening wine," is taken from Jeremiah 25. It means the religious *experts* from the world's seven religious systems will advocate a solution to appease God which is totally false. They will not understand God's Word and will not listen to the 144,000. So, they will offer a solution that actually opposes almighty God! The political leaders, not knowing what to do, will swallow the false solution (maddening wine) "hook, line, and sinker." The result will be religious and political chaos. The effect is similar to people drinking too much wine and becoming unable to reason or think clearly.

Babylon will severely punish millions of innocent people (saints). When religious leaders and political leaders unite, nothing good comes from it, because the union of church and state is an adulterous union in God's sight. Fearing more judgments are imminent, political leaders will go along with the religious experts and a ferocious worldwide religious-police state will appear demanding compliance. These religious police will be similar to the Islamic *mutawa*, but much more ruthless.

The second message to the world will be religiously and politically inflammatory. It will put the ministry of the 144,000, and those who embrace their ministry, in direct opposition to the world leaders' agenda. The 144,000 will proclaim Jesus is almighty God and the seventh day of the week is His holy Sabbath. Most of the world will defy the first two messages. Even the Jews, who recognize the seventh day as holy, will resist the testimony of the 144,000 because the Jews will strenuously oppose the declaration that Jesus Christ is

1   Revelation 14:8, insertions mine

almighty God. Likewise, Muslims, Catholics, and Protestants will strenuously oppose the holiness of the seventh day.

The second message will be a universal call, sent from Jesus to the people of Earth, to separate themselves from their religious and political heritage which support the mission and goal of the seven-headed beast. This call will separate the faith-full from the faith-less.

The Third Message

After a period of about two years (as I calculate it), most of the inhabitants of Earth will have made a decision regarding the first two messages. The gospel proclaimed by the 144,000 will stall. The fifth trumpet will then occur, **"Because they refused to love the truth and so be saved. For this reason God sends them a powerful delusion so that they will believe the lie and so that all will be condemned who have not believed the truth but have delighted in wickedness."**[1]

It is ironic to realize that man's efforts to reduce global wickedness will only cause it to increase! After Jesus releases the devil and his demons from the Abyss, a third message will be given. **"A third angel followed them** [the previous two angels, flying in midair] **and said in a loud voice** [to the inhabitants on Earth below]: **'If anyone worships the beast** [the great red dragon that comes up out of the Abyss. The appearing of the devil is also described in Revelation 13:11-18 as a beast coming up out of the earth. This beast is the Antichrist, the devil, the man of lawlessness, the great red dragon who was thrown out of heaven. He will be released from the spirit realm at the fifth trumpet as "a powerful delusion." This message is a serious warning: If anyone worships the beast] **and its image** [that is, if anyone worships the devil as God and participates in his theocracy] **and receives its mark** [the Greek word, *charagma*, which means an engraving, etching, or tattoo] **on their forehead or on their hand, they, too, will drink the wine of God's fury, which has been poured full strength into the cup of his wrath. They will**

---

1   2 Thessalonians 2:10-12

be tormented with burning sulfur in the presence of the holy angels and of the Lamb.' "[1]

The third message will light up the world because the angel speaks with "a loud voice!" The third message will be a warning from Jesus stating the consequences for worshiping the Antichrist. This will be a very difficult time. If a person worships the devil, he will receive the wrath of God. If he worships Jesus, he will receive the wrath of the devil! This third message will make the devil and his demons furious with the 144,000 and their followers. Therefore, the devil—the beast from the Abyss—will kill most, if not all, of the 144,000 as quickly as possible.

The Fourth Message

Five months later, during the period of the sixth trumpet, a final message will be sent to the inhabitants of Earth. This message will impact the whole world even more than the previous messages! Jesus wants to save sinners. This final message is designed to rescue anyone who is in turmoil about what to do. Some people may have received the mark of the beast out of fear, but they have not yet committed the unpardonable sin. In other words, some people may take the mark of the beast and then regret doing so. This message is for such people: **"After this I saw another angel coming down from heaven. He had great authority, and the earth was illuminated by his splendor. With a mighty voice he shouted: ' "Fallen! Fallen is Babylon the Great!" She has become a dwelling for demons and a haunt** [a dwelling place] **for every impure spirit, a haunt for every unclean bird, a haunt for every unclean and detestable animal. For all the nations have drunk the maddening wine of her adulteries. The kings of the earth committed adultery with her, and the merchants of the earth grew rich from her excessive luxuries.' Then I heard another voice from heaven say:** [at this point, Jesus will speak from heaven to the people on Earth through the mouths of the 144,000. Jesus is calling out those who have been afraid to put their faith in Him:] **'Come out of her** [the whore in

---

1 Revelation 14:9-10, insertions mine

Revelation 17, the devil's theocracy, come out], *my people,* **so that you will not share in her sins, so that you will not receive any of her plagues; for her sins are piled up to heaven, and God has remembered her crimes. Give back to her as she has given; pay her back double for what she has done. Pour her a double portion from her own cup.'** "[1]

The Sixth Trumpet

Now that we have discussed the four testing messages given by the 144,000, let us go back in time to the fifth trumpet. After five months of world travel and deception, many people will refuse to worship the devil as almighty God. A large component of this group will be the nonreligious wicked. When the sixth trumpet occurs, the devil will suddenly cease to be a "very wonderful and gracious God" for those who have chosen to follow him. Overnight he will morph into a cruel dictator because he will receive permission from Jesus to kill one third of mankind. Remember the story of Job when the devil was allowed to kill Job's children. The devil will give orders and anyone refusing to obey will be subject to death. He will abolish the religions and governments of the world in order to establish himself as the undisputed "King of kings and Lord of lords." As he reorganizes his domain, the whole world will become agitated, and a great war will ensue between those who believe the devil is Almighty God and nonreligious people who refuse to obey the Antichrist. John saw this war, and you need to understand it to appreciate the purpose and timing of the mark of the beast.

Some people cannot accept the idea that Jesus would give the devil permission to kill one third of mankind; but killing people is not out of character for almighty God. Revelation 19 indicates that at the Second Coming, Jesus Himself will kill His enemies with a command as represented by a sharp sword that comes out of His mouth.[2] Keep in mind that Jesus is the same God who killed 25% of the earth's inhabitants with the first four trumpets. Our Creator also

---

1   Revelation 18:1-6, insertions and italics mine
2   Revelation 19:15

killed everyone outside the ark in Noah's flood, all of the firstborn in Egypt who did not have blood on the doorposts, and 185,000 of Sennacherib's soldiers in one night![1]

At the time of the sixth trumpet, the world will be mostly divided into two distinct groups of people: the saints and the enemies of Jesus. Whether the devil kills the enemies of Jesus or Jesus Himself kills His enemies, there is no difference. Jesus also breaks the fifth seal at the sixth trumpet. This means that during the slaughter of the sixth trumpet, many saints will also perish. Jesus permits many of His saints to die as martyrs so, if possible, the few who are not fully decided may be saved. **"Come out of her, my people!"**[2] The strongest testimony a saint can give for Jesus is his life. **"They** [the saints] **triumphed over him** [the beast, the great red dragon] **by the blood of the Lamb and by the word of their testimony; they did not love their lives so much as to shrink from death."**[3]

"The sixth angel sounded his trumpet, and I heard a voice coming from the four horns of the golden altar [of Incense] **that is before God."**[4] The Altar of Incense was used in the earthly tabernacle to represent corporate intercession. Corporate intercession was conducted each day because God wanted to teach Israel that life on Earth was only possible because sinners had an intercessor. When Adam and Eve sinned, they were supposed to have been killed on the very day they had eaten the fruit.[5] When Jesus agreed to the Father's plan of salvation, Jesus became man's intercessor. Jesus placed himself between the demand of the law (death) and the guilty pair as their shield (intercessor). Subsequently, Jesus has been shielding all sinners for 6,000 years.

John heard an angel speak from the Altar of Incense at the sixth trumpet, indicating that Jesus' intercession is about to end forever. When the sixth trumpet is completed, Jesus will release His wrath

---

1   Isaiah 37:36
2   Revelation 18:4
3   Revelation 12:11, insertions mine
4   Revelation 9:13, insertion mine
5   Genesis 2:17

(seven bowls) without mercy on the wicked. After the thousand years are over, the wicked then will be resurrected to die the second death in hell.

"It [the voice at the Altar of Incense] **said to the sixth angel who had the trumpet, 'Release the four angels who are bound at the great river Euphrates.' "**[1] This language has roots in the geography of ancient Israel. The great river Euphrates was a natural boundary for the northern border of Israel. Each spring the Euphrates River flooded from melting snow and the rushing river kept kings and armies from invading Israel from the north. In Bible times, it was also understood that divine judgment came, "out of the north."[2] This understanding was perhaps based on the idea that God's throne was located on the north side of the temple. Speaking of the devil's ambition, Isaiah wrote, **"For thou hast said in thine heart, I will ascend into heaven, I will exalt my throne above the stars of God: I will sit also upon the mount of the congregation, in the sides of the north."**[3]

At the sixth trumpet, the release of four angels which were bound at the north border, held back by the great river Euphrates, means a divine judgment is coming. There will be no further protection from the Antichrist and his demons. Remember, during the fifth trumpet, the devil and his demons were not permitted to kill anyone, but only allowed to torment the wicked.

"And the four angels who had been kept ready for this very hour and day and month and year were released to kill a third of mankind."[4] Long ago, the Father set the date to the very hour, for the sixth trumpet. This indicates God's mercy for sinners is not endless. God's probation for sinners has a deadline. I anticipate the sixth trumpet will last a little more than seven months. During this time, the devil will be permitted to kill one third of mankind. The Antichrist will gladly do this as he establishes his throne and theocracy.

1   Revelation 9:14, insertion mine
2   Jeremiah 4:5-6; 25:9; Isaiah 41:25; Ezekiel 1:4; 38:15; Daniel 11:36; Job 37:22
3   Isaiah 14:13, KJV
4   Revelation 9:15

"The number of the mounted troops was twice ten thousand times ten thousand. I heard their number."[1] Some translations say 200 hundred million troops. Currently, the number of standing troops from all nations is less than 20 million. The devil will be able to create and supply an army that is ten times larger in a short time because he will offer everyone volunteering to serve him a position of authority in his kingdom and generous rations. Since the 144,000 will withhold the rain[2] and global famine caused by the fourth trumpet will be ongoing, millions of starving people will gladly join the devil's army. The devil will use a deceptive offer to entice people to annihilate his enemies. After the satanic army has done his bidding, the antichrist will betray his volunteers and have them killed because of insufficient rations. Many nonreligious people will resist the devil's efforts to establish his throne and worldwide church-state (theocracy). This will lead to a worldwide civil war, brothers fighting against brothers in every nation.

John saw the battle: **"The horses and riders I saw in my vision looked like this: Their breastplates were fiery red, dark blue, and yellow as sulfur. The heads of the horses resembled the heads of lions, and out of their mouths came fire, smoke and sulfur. A third of mankind was killed by the three plagues of fire, smoke and sulfur that came out of their mouths. The power of the horses was in their mouths and in their tails; for their tails were like snakes, having heads with which they inflict injury."**[3]

John used metaphors to describe this vision. In John's day, when armies from different cities and tribal nations assembled together against a common foe, the soldiers did not know one another. Therefore, soldiers wore similar bright colors so that in the fog of battle, they could quickly distinguish between friend and foe. The same idea applies here. The devil's military will not be a standing army in uniform; there is no money or time for equipping an army of 200 million troops. The Antichrist's armies will largely consist of

1   Revelation 9:16
2   Revelation 11:6
3   Revelation 9:17-19

civilians who rallied and joined up with the devil for authority and rations – only to discover at the end, the devil lied.

John also saw very strange but powerful horses in his vision. God used this imagery so that we can understand this battle will be incredibly brutal. Every weapon created by man will be used. Cities will be left in ruins. The world will be a wilderness. No wonder Isaiah wrote, **"Is this the man who shook the earth and made kingdoms tremble, the man who made the world a wilderness, who overthrew its cities?"**[1] The man of lawlessness and his demons will rejoice when they see men and women tearing each other apart, treating one another with demon-inspired hatred and cruelty.

"The rest of mankind who were not killed by these plagues still did not repent of the work of their hands; they did not stop worshiping demons, and idols of gold, silver, bronze, stone and wood–idols that cannot see or hear or walk. Nor did they repent of their murders, their magic arts, their sexual immorality or their thefts."[2]

These final two sentences of the sixth trumpet reveal the failure, foolishness, and stupidity of the seven-headed beast. Nothing stops a sinner from sinning if he does not first have a change of heart and mind. Persecution and punishment only drives a determined sinner to circumvent obstacles.

Considering the impact of the first four trumpets; the work and ministry of the 144,000 for 1,260 days; the tenacious effort of the Holy Spirit to win each heart; the testimony of Jesus; the great enlightenment period; God's generous offer to seal and save each repentant sinner; and then, in contrast, the brutality and atrocities committed by the Antichrist, it "boggles the mind." Surprisingly, there is no change in the behavior of the wicked.

By the end of the sixth trumpet, Jesus will have done everything possible to save each sinner and each person will have made a

---

1   Isaiah 14:16-17
2   Revelation 9:20-21

decision. When Jesus determines extended mercy has no redeeming effect, He will close the door to salvation with this benediction: **"Let the one who does wrong continue to do wrong; let the vile person continue to be vile; let the one who does right continue to do right; and let the holy person continue to be holy."**[1]

Satan's Throne and Tattoo

Remember, when Jesus grants the devil permission to kill one third of mankind, Satan will become a ruthless dictator. He will abolish the religions and governments of the world. He will throw religious and political leaders "under the bus" and divide Earth[2] into ten sectors led by ten "puppet kings."[3] Incidentally, these kings are represented by the ten horns on the seven-headed beast.[4] The devil will give them the task of building his "kingdom of God."

The devil will decree everyone must work if they want to eat. The sick, elderly, and injured will be left to die.

Because he will be opposed to all that is worshiped or called "God," I believe the devil will change the weekly cycle and declare a new day as his holy day. If true, it will accomplish two goals. First, for all mankind, there will be no further controversy over which day is holy. "God" has spoken and when God lives among mankind, there is no room for religious or political diversity. Second, by changing the weekly cycle, those who honor the Sabbath of the Creator will be easy to identify because they will not work on the Lord's seventh day Sabbath. The devil's primary motive will be to expose all "Sabbath keepers" so he can destroy them. **"The second beast** [the Antichrist] **was given power** [from Jesus at the sixth trumpet] **to give breath** [authority] **to the image of the first beast** [the devil's theocracy], **so that the image could speak and cause all who refused to worship the image** [obey the laws of the theocracy] **to be killed."**[5]

---

1   Revelation 22:11
2   Daniel 11:39
3   Daniel 2:44
4   Revelation 13:1; 17:12-13
5   Revelation 13:15, insertions mine

The devil will resort to an ancient method for dealing with large numbers of people to manage his subjects in this extreme and rapidly deteriorating environment. He will require his puppet kings to divide their subjects into groups of one thousand.[1] One person will be chosen from each group to serve as its captain. After the divisions are made, each captain will be told to tell his group that the first 666 people willing to step forward and receive a tattoo on the right hand showing "666" will receive rations. The others will be put to death. This decree will create the global civil war described in the sixth trumpet. This is why and how one third of mankind will be killed.

Mathematically, 999 people minus 333 (one third) people equals 666 people. This horrible and gruesome tactic will expose and eliminate those who have the slightest reservation about worshiping the devil and obeying his laws. Those who rush forward will be rewarded with a tattoo which allows them to obtain rations.

The phrase "the mark of the beast" is a popular, but poor, translation from the Greek language. The phrase should be translated "the engraving of the beast." The Greek word "charagma" is translated "mark" in English Bibles, but the word means an engraving, such as an engraving on a tombstone or in the flesh, a tattoo, or brand. Tattooing requires embedding pigment under the skin, and branding requires a hot iron to sear the skin. Both are simple, low-tech, easy procedures to control people in large numbers. Hitler tattooed millions of prisoners living in primitive conditions, and the devil will do the same. A tattoo/brand is not subject to theft or counterfeiting and is not reversible or transferable. It does not require electricity. A tattoo/brand showing "666" on the right hand will be required to conduct business during the rare opportunities possible. The dire circumstances on Earth at the time of the sixth trumpet force this draconian action. Each captain overseeing one thousand will also wear an indelible mark on his forehead to signal

---

1   See examples of this in Exodus 18:24-26, Numbers 31:48-54, Deuteronomy 1:15, 1 Samuel 22:7, and 1 Chronicles 27:1.

his rank. From ancient times, field-grade military officers have worn various flourishes on their hats so that everyone can see when a high level official is approaching or present.

The devil will delightfully execute one third of mankind because killing them will intimidate the survivors. Everyone will tremble, seeing that the "fierce-looking king"[1] has absolute control over life and death. Those receiving the devil's tattoo will be reminded that they can only live for as long as they worship and obey their demonic master! Killing one third of mankind also insures life on Earth can last a little longer. Sustaining people in misery will only increase the devil's sadistic nature because he can torment his subjects for an extended period of time. His pleasure is in wielding demonic power over his subjects. The devil is sick, rabid, and powerful. Therefore, the devil will take great pleasure when he receives permission from Jesus to kill one third of mankind. His depth of twisted cruelty and hatred for God and man is impossible to comprehend. The Great Tribulation will be painful, deeply affecting every survivor.

The Evil Imposter

Whatever Jesus intends to do, the Antichrist will imitate. Jesus will kill two billion people (25% of eight billion people); the devil will kill two billion people (33% of six billion people). Jesus made the seventh day holy at Creation; the Antichrist will declare a holy day. Jesus will have a mere 144,000 prophets speaking for Him; the devil will have ten times more. Jesus will warn the inhabitants of Earth that anyone worshiping the Antichrist will be destroyed; the Antichrist will tell the world that anyone refusing to worship him will be destroyed.

As Jesus will appear in clouds of glory at His Second Coming and every eye will see Him as Earth rotates beneath His throne, the Antichrist and his demons will try to imitate Jesus and descend from the sky with a great show of glory and power. However, unlike Jesus who does not touch the earth because the saints are caught up to meet the Lord in the air, the Antichrist and his demons will repeartedly

---

1   Daniel 8:23

descend in many places to deceive the inhabitants of Earth, and to establish his throne and kingdom. Jesus will abolish the religions and governments of the world through His gospel. The devil will establish his theocracy through brute force and a global war.

Finally, Jesus will require and provide the seal of God for everyone who obeys the everlasting gospel and puts their faith in Him; the Antichrist will require everyone permitted to live to bear his tattoo or brand. Those receiving the devil's indelible mark will suffer during the seven bowls and die when Jesus appears. Those receiving the seal of God will not be affected by the seven bowls, although many saints will die and sleep through the seven bowls. A few saints will live through it all. **"Blessed is the one who waits for and reaches the end of the 1,335 days."**[1]

Identifying the Antichrist

The Bible reveals many details about the coming Antichrist. It is a huge story with many threads. Let us review the following concepts and, more importantly, do not forget them:

1. Identity of the Antichrist as the man of lawlessness

2. About two billion people are killed during the first four trumpets (judgments)

3. World's religious and political leaders have a knee-jerk response to appease God's wrath

4. Three convenient lies to justify creating the seven-headed beast

5. Purpose and reach of the seven-headed beast, the crisis government

6. Seven-headed beast which is seven "governors" leading seven different ways to appease one God

7. Hardship endured before the Antichrist is released from the Abyss at the fifth trumpet

---

1 Daniel 12:12

8. Jesus releases the Antichrist from the spirit realm and permits him to appear "in the flesh"

9. The devil appears after there is a great rebellion against truth, when the gospel has stalled

10. Antichrist will perform amazing miracles and proclaim himself to be God

11. Antichrist is opposed to all religions; he cannot align with one without alienating the others

12. Three lies conceived by religious leaders will align perfectly with the devil's lies

13. Antichrist objectives of "rule and ruin"

14. Exaltation of Jesus in 1798 as Almighty God

15. A period of great enlightenment consisting of four messages

16. First message: Fear God, worship the Creator, judgment has begun

17. Global conflict will arise over the deity of Jesus and His Sabbath

18. Second message: Babylon's efforts to appease God's wrath are blasphemous to God

19. Third message: Jesus will destroy anyone whe worships the Antichrist

20. Fourth message: Last call, come out of Babylon to escape her guilt

21. Devil is given permission to kill one third of mankind at the sixth trumpet

22. Devil abolishes all the world's religions and governments to rule as king and lord

23. Devil offers rations to all who receive his tattoo

24. Antichrist divides the world into ten sectors and appoints ten puppet kings

25. Survivors will be divided into groups of one thousand

26. Global civil war breaks out because nonreligious people refuse to obey and worship the Antichrist

27. Antichrist will imitate a Jesus that most of the world does not know and imitate everything Jesus intends to do

When valid rules of interpretation are used to interpret apocalyptic prophecy, this is the story that Daniel and Revelation produce. God has set the hour, day, month, and year of the fifth trumpet when the Antichrist will appear. God has not revealed the date, but we have clues indicating when this event will occur. God intends to surprise the wicked with the devil's appearing because they willingly and knowingly refused to love the truth and be saved. When man's rebellion has exhausted God's patience, God will release and reveal the man of lawlessness. The prophet Daniel wrote about this: **"In the latter part of their reign, when rebels have become completely wicked, a fierce-looking, a master of intrigue, will arise. He will become very strong, but not by his own power. He will cause astounding devastation and will succeed in whatever he does. He will destroy those who are mighty, the holy people."**[1]

The devil will appear on Earth in the form of a man, but he will not be an ordinary man. He will be a lawless man who opposes and abolishes the governments and religions of the world to set up a counterfeit theocracy, his own government and religion. He will reign as King of kings and Lord of lords for a short time, because God has given him permission to rule over and destroy the whole earth. John says the devil's **"name in Hebrew is Abaddon and in Greek is Apollyon (that is, Destroyer)."**[2] Isaiah says he will turn the world into a wilderness.

---

1   Daniel 8:23-24
2   Revelation 9:11

The time has come for speculation to end. Present truth has appeared. The Bible says clearly: The Antichrist is the devil, also called Satan. He is the angel king from the Abyss (spirit realm). He will appear in the form of a man, but will be no ordinary man. He will be lawless. He will set up his own government and religion and rule over the whole earth.[1] He is a destroyer and will turn the world into a wilderness.

A great enlightenment is coming and a great rebellion will follow. During this rebellion, the Antichrist will appear. He will be the world's worst nightmare, killing one third of mankind! Remember, when a group of people become defiant and God determines that extended mercy will have no redeeming effect, He sends destruction.

I wish this story were not true. I do not like what the Bible predicts about tomorrow. I do, however, love what the Bible says about the "day after tomorrow"—spending eternity with the Father, the Son, the Holy Spirit, and all the saints. Until then, I pray this book about the Antichrist awakens your interest and prompts you to intensify your Bible study efforts.

Ready or not, believe it or not, like it or not, the end of all things is near. Prepare to meet Jesus by living a life that is pleasing to Him. Surrender your life to Him each day. Worship Jesus, give Him glory! Keep His Sabbath day holy by resting from your labors. Spend the Sabbath in Bible study and prayer, visiting and spiritually encouraging others. If you struggle with a known sin, confess it to Jesus and ask Him to send the power of the Holy Spirit to overcome the sin. Make past wrongs right as far as possible. And lastly, share this message, book, and our website with friends and family so they too will not be deceived by a miracle-working Antichrist. God's people have a King and Redeemer. The wicked do not know it yet, but they also have a king who is the destroyer of souls. Choose carefully whom you will serve—Christ or the Antichrist. We each actually do serve one or the other. I pray you will prepare for the fulfillment of God's Word by filling your mind with God's Word!

1   Daniel 11:36

This book has examined important facts about the coming Antichrist and is based on material published on our website. To study further, visit our website at *wake-up.org* to read other studies and browse the many topics available. If you read something in this book which is new to you, support material which may answer your questions is available at the link.

If this book has been helpful and you would like to share it, we will be pleased to send free copies of this book while supplies last provided you pay shipping and handling (limits and intervals also apply).

May God bless you as you study this fascinating topic!

Wake Up America Seminars, Inc.
P.O. Box 273
Bellbrook, OH 45305
wake-up.org
email: *wuaseminars@gmail.com*

About the Author

Larry Wilson became a born-again Christian after returning from Vietnam. His understanding of the gospel, the plan of salvation, and the atonement of Jesus Christ thrilled his soul his entire life. He spent over 40 years intensely studying the prophecies of Daniel and Revelation. In 1988, he published his first book and during his lifetime, wrote many other books. Over one million books are in circulation throughout the world.

About the Organization

Wake Up America Seminars (WUAS) is both a nonprofit and nondenominational organization. With God's blessings and the generosity of many people, WUAS has distributed millions of pamphlets, books, and tapes around the world since it began in 1988. WUAS is not a church and is not affiliated or sponsored by any religious organization. It promotes the primacy of salvation through faith in Jesus Christ, His imminent return, and is doing its best to encourage people with the good news of the gospel.

We encourage you to visit our website for further study. Most of the study materials that Larry Wilson produced during his 40 years of ministry are available for free at *wake-up.org*.

If you have comments about this book or questions, please send them to the email or physical address below.

Wake Up America Seminars, Inc.
P.O. Box 273
Bellbrook, OH 45305
wake-up.org
email: *wuaseminars@gmail.com*